Lecture Notes in Economics and Mathematical Systems

674

Founding Editors:

M. Beckmann
H.P. Künzi

Managing Editors:

Prof. Dr. G. Fandel
Fachbereich Wirtschaftswissenschaften
Fernuniversität Hagen
Hagen, Germany

Prof. Dr. W. Trockel
Murat Sertel Institute for Advanced Economic Research
Istanbul Bilgi University
Istanbul, Turkey

and

Institut für Mathematische Wirtschaftsforschung (IMW)
Universität Bielefeld
Bielefeld, Germany

Editorial Board:

H. Dawid, D. Dimitrov, A. Gerber, C-J. Haake, C. Hofmann, T. Pfeiffer,
R. Słowiński, W.H.M. Zijm

For further volumes:
http://www.springer.com/series/300

Daniel Gartner

Optimizing Hospital-wide Patient Scheduling

Early Classification of Diagnosis-related Groups Through Machine Learning

 Springer

Daniel Gartner
TUM School of Management
Technische Universität München
München
Germany

Dissertation at the Technische Universität München, TUM School of Management, submitted on June 12th, 2013 and accepted on July 15th, 2013

ISSN 0075-8442
ISBN 978-3-319-04065-3   ISBN 978-3-319-04066-0 (eBook)
DOI 10.1007/978-3-319-04066-0
Springer Cham Heidelberg New York Dordrecht London

Library of Congress Control Number: 2014931786

© Springer International Publishing Switzerland 2014
This work is subject to copyright. All rights are reserved by the Publisher, whether the whole or part of the material is concerned, specifically the rights of translation, reprinting, reuse of illustrations, recitation, broadcasting, reproduction on microfilms or in any other physical way, and transmission or information storage and retrieval, electronic adaptation, computer software, or by similar or dissimilar methodology now known or hereafter developed. Exempted from this legal reservation are brief excerpts in connection with reviews or scholarly analysis or material supplied specifically for the purpose of being entered and executed on a computer system, for exclusive use by the purchaser of the work. Duplication of this publication or parts thereof is permitted only under the provisions of the Copyright Law of the Publisher's location, in its current version, and permission for use must always be obtained from Springer. Permissions for use may be obtained through RightsLink at the Copyright Clearance Center. Violations are liable to prosecution under the respective Copyright Law.
The use of general descriptive names, registered names, trademarks, service marks, etc. in this publication does not imply, even in the absence of a specific statement, that such names are exempt from the relevant protective laws and regulations and therefore free for general use.
While the advice and information in this book are believed to be true and accurate at the date of publication, neither the authors nor the editors nor the publisher can accept any legal responsibility for any errors or omissions that may be made. The publisher makes no warranty, express or implied, with respect to the material contained herein.

Printed on acid-free paper

Springer is part of Springer Science+Business Media (www.springer.com)

Acknowledgements

First and foremost, I would like to thank Prof. Dr. Rainer Kolisch, who offered me a research position at the TUM School of Management, provided me a highly interesting research topic and supported me in every aspect of my research. Furthermore, my gratitude goes to Prof. Rema Padman, PhD, and Prof. Daniel Bertrand Neill, PhD, who offered me the opportunity to collaborate on research at the Heinz College, Carnegie Mellon University, USA. I would like to thank in particular Prof. Rema Padman, PhD, for joining the dissertation committee and Prof. Dr. Gunther Friedl for chairing it.

I am very grateful to Dr. Dirk Last and Martin Kornhaas of the county hospital Erding for contributing their clinical experience to my research and for providing the data for the case studies.

I would like to offer my thanks to former and current colleagues at the department: Claus Henning Brech, Prof. Dr. Jens Otto Brunner, Dr. André Dahlmann, Jia Yan Du, Thomas Fliedner, Markus Matthäus Frey, Dr. Andreas Fügener, Dr. Christian Heimerl, Ferdinand Kiermaier, Dr. Philipp Melchiors, Anulark Naber, PhD, Sebastian Schiffels and Dr. Hans-Jörg Schütz for many valuable discussions. Moreover, I am grateful to Stephen Starck, PhD, from the TUM language center for his valuable feedback on academic writing.

Finally, I want to thank Ines Verena Arnolds and my family for their invaluable support.

Munich, Germany   Daniel Gartner
June 2013

Contents

List of Figures

List of Tables

Chapter 1
Introduction

The introductory chapter consists of five sections. Section 1.1 highlights different aspects of the economic situation in hospitals. In particular, it describes the reimbursement system wherein hospitals are financed by insurances for inpatient care, based on diagnosis-related groups (DRGs). Section 1.2 explains the necessity of planning the inpatient flow in a holistic way. It outlines the need for providing health care efficiently for a variety of inpatients, each having individual characteristics and requirements for multiple types of scarce resources. Section 1.3 presents the different managerial areas and hierarchical decision levels in hospitals and classifies the problem of optimizing the hospital-wide flow of elective patients addressed in this dissertation. Section 1.4 emphasizes the importance of accurately classifying the DRG for each patient and why it is necessary to develop an optimization approach for the DRG-based scheduling of inpatients. The research questions are introduced and a structured and comprehensive approach to answering these questions is given. The chapter closes with a presentation of the dissertation outline in Sect. 1.5.

1.1 DRG-Systems and the Economic Situation in Hospitals

For many years, cost reimbursement has been the standard payment scheme for hospitals. In this scheme, a hospital receives the total cost for treating the patient which is calculated by multiplying the patient's length of stay (LOS) with a (ward specific) daily rate and adding the costs for clinical procedures applied, such as X-ray diagnostics and surgery. Cost reimbursement does not provide an incentive for hospitals to operate efficiently. As a consequence, hospital costs as the largest part of total health care costs (approximately 31 % in the U.S., see Lim et al. [125]), have increased sharply. In an effort to limit hospital costs and to create an incentive for hospitals to operate more efficiently, many countries have introduced payment schemes that are based on DRGs. Schreyögg et al. [194] provide an overview of the evolution of different DRG-systems in different nations. Since the publication of their work in 2006, several other countries have introduced DRGs as a reimbursement system (see Table 3.8) while most recently, Switzerland has introduced DRGs in 2012.

In DRG-based reimbursement schemes, patients are classified into DRGs with homogeneous clinical characteristics and resources required during treatment within each group, while between groups, the patients' clinical characteristics and therefore costs are different. Hospitals receive payments based on the DRG instead of the applied procedures and the LOS. The reimbursement for treating a patient with a specific DRG equals the average cost which accrued in a representative sample of hospitals in the year before last. For each country, there is an institution, such as the German institute for the reimbursement in hospitals (InEK, see Schreyögg et al. [195]), responsible for generating the sample, collecting, processing and distributing the cost data.

With DRG-based payment schemes in place, in order to be profitable, a hospital has to operate such that its patient specific costs are lower than the average costs of the hospitals in the sample. However, the cost structure in hospitals, as in many service industries, is such that the predominant share of the operational costs is fixed. Hence, costs can only be marginally reduced by operational decisions. Thus, hospitals have to use existing resources such that revenue or the total contribution margin is maximized. This approach is well-known in the service industry (see Kimes [101] for an example in the service industry in general as well as Schütz and Kolisch [196] for an example in the health care industry in particular).

DRGs can be used by hospitals in two ways: For accounting and for operations management. The goal of the accounting-driven DRG classification is to group inpatients by DRG for billing and reimbursement purposes, using all clinical and demographic information available once the inpatient is discharged from the hospital. Typically, a simple, flowchart-based method, which is implemented in a commercial software and called "DRG grouper", is used for this task. Figure 1.1 illustrates the DRG-grouping.

Before the execution of the DRG grouper, parameter values, such as the primary diagnosis, secondary diagnoses, clinical procedures, age, gender as well as weight in the case of newborns have to be entered into the software. Diagnoses are coded by using the international statistical classification of diseases and related health problems (ICD). The first three levels of ICD codes correspond to DRGs. The algorithm first determines 1 of 23 major diagnostic categories (MDC). Those are in particular defined by the primary diagnosis (i.e. the reason for the hospitalization). However, if the primary diagnosis is imprecisely documented, an error DRG will be returned. On the contrary, if the patient has e.g. a transplantation, a Pre-MDC (a DRG with high-cost procedures, see Busse et al. [29]) is returned. After determining the MDC, clinical procedures and co-morbidities lead to the patient's DRG which can be categorized into surgical, medical and other DRGs. Finally, within these categories, the age of the patient or the weight in the case of newborns may lead to a different DRG-subtype. Mathematically, the assignment of a patient to a DRG is a surjective function since each patient is assigned exactly one of

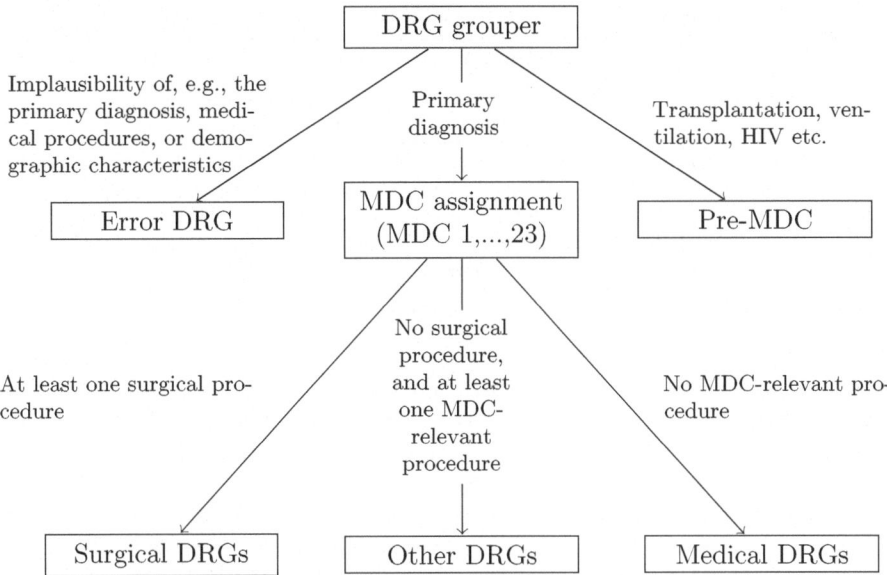

Fig. 1.1 Hierarchical DRG-grouping process (See Schreyögg et al. [195])

the 1,154 possible DRGs (in the German DRG system of 2010, see Porter and Guth [172]). Conversely, one DRG can be assigned to two different patients who may have different diagnoses, coded by the ICD.

Operations-driven DRG classification is performed at earlier stages of care in order to facilitate the planning of health care operations. For example, the current approach of the hospital where this study was undertaken, is to classify the DRG of the inpatient not earlier than 1 day after admission. It is assumed that, after the first day, the hospital's information about the inpatient is sufficiently complete to accurately compute the DRG, and thus the DRG grouper is used to consolidate the available information to a "working DRG". Based on this DRG, further information such as costs, revenue and the clinical pathway can be derived and used for planning purposes. However, the existing DRG grouper is ill-suited for the operations-driven DRG prediction task because it assumes that the inpatient's current lists of diagnoses and treatments are complete and will not change over the remainder of the inpatient's hospital stay. In fact, new health conditions may arise or be identified during the stay, and additional procedures may be performed in response, necessitating a change in the inpatient's DRG and substantially affecting the hospital's revenues, costs and resource allocations. One can argue that many such changes follow regular patterns, and that these patterns can be learned from inpatient data, thus improving the prediction of the inpatient's DRG in the early stages of their hospital visit.

Having determined the DRG of a discharged patient, one can determine revenue, which is both a function of the patient's DRG and his LOS. However, in order to

Table 1.1 Top-level classification of cost elements and cost centers

		Cost elements			
				Infrastructure	
		Personnel	Material	Medical	Non-medical
Cost centers	Hospital units with beds	Intensive care time, nursing time	Medication costs	Nursing days	Nursing days
	Diagnostic and treatment areas	Incision to closure time	Balloon catheter	Sterilization oxygen	Washing cleaning

compute the contribution margin, which is dependent on the DRG and the LOS as well, decision relevant costs also have to be taken into account. Table 1.1 provides an aggregated overview of the cost elements and the cost centers in a hospital (see [3]). Hospital units with beds are, e.g., intensive care units (ICU) whereas diagnostic and treatment areas may be the surgery room. Personnel costs include nursing time, among others. Since the optimization approach that will be presented later should not be used to make medical decisions, the non-medical infrastructure costs of hospital units with beds are decision relevant. For example, whether or not a patient should have a balloon catheter instead of some other catheter type, or any catheter at all, is not decision relevant. However, "hotel costs" which occur, e.g., for washing and cleaning *are* decision relevant and dependent on LOS. For an example of the revenue, cost and contribution margin functions, see Fig. 3.1.

1.2   Necessity of a Holistic Planning Approach

Scheduling patients in a hospital with the objective of maximizing the contribution margin, based on DRG and LOS, can only be done in a holistic way which will be outlined in the following. Therefore, four different dimensions that comprise holistic planning will be presented: Patients (demand), resources (supply), relations between patients and clinical activities, and uncertainty. First of all, when focusing on patients, a variety of possible clinical pathways exist in hospitals. A clinical pathway can be understood as a standardized, typically evidence based health care process (see van De Klundert et al. [224]). For an example of clinical pathways, see Fig. 3.2. Figure 1.2 presents a schedule of a surgical (a) and a therapeutical clinical pathway (b) as Gantt diagrams where CT denotes computer tomography. The schedules suggest that the different types of clinical pathways require the second holistic planning dimension, namely multiple resource types. A diagnostic activity for instance requires diagnostic resources, while a patient's admission activity allocates a bed, usually for several nights until discharge. The figure also reveals that the third holistic planning dimension has to be taken into account since, from a temporal view, a patient's activities may not start before another patient's

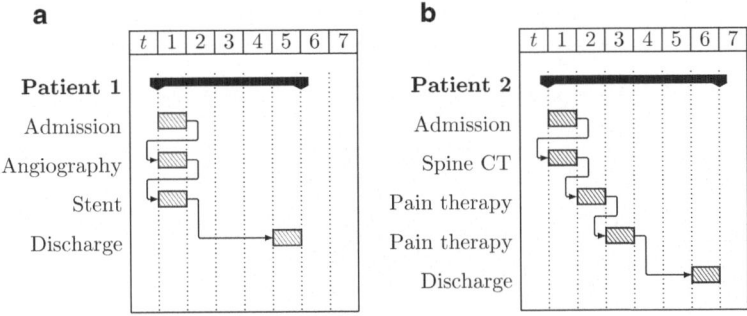

Fig. 1.2   A schedule for a surgical (**a**) and therapeutical clinical pathway (**b**)

activities are finished. Finally, several sources of uncertainty, such as uncertain recovery times, may arise during the execution of the schedule.

As stated above, the DRG of a patient is determined at discharge, after all demographic and clinical information about the patient has been collected and documented. In order to schedule patients with the objective to maximize contribution margin, the challenge is however, to classify the DRG for each patient already at the point in time when the patient contacts the hospital for admission. The question, which attributes are relevant and how these attributes should be connected to a classification approach is the challenge of the machine learning problem addressed in this dissertation. Linking these DRGs to the hospital-wide scheduling of the patient flow is the aim of this dissertation's holistic planning.

1.3   Strategic, Tactical and Operational Problems in Hospitals

Secondary literature on and a discussion of frameworks for the planning and the control of resources in hospitals is available in Hans et al. [84]. The authors introduce a general framework which is shown in Table 1.2. The rows contain the elements of Anthony's classification [10]. The columns represent the different managerial areas of a hospital. One can find studies that can be categorized into each row and column. Observe the diagonal row from the lower left to the upper right. Triage, for example, is treated in Iserson and Moskop [93]. They study the historical development of triage systems. Conforti et al. [46] is an example for patient scheduling. They provide a scheduling model for patients in a week hospital environment. The article will be discussed in more detail in Chap. 3. An example for supplier selection is Lambert et al. [112] who found out that for purchasing managers in hospitals, costs are of relatively low importance for supplier selection, compared to the supplier's service and delivery. Finally, Zelman et al. [243] is a textbook for the financial management of health care organizations.

Table 1.2 Framework for hospital planning and control (see Hans et al. [84])

	Medical planning	Resource capacity planning	Materials planning	Financial planning
Strategic	Research, development of medical protocols	Case mix planning, capacity dimensioning	Supply chain and warehouse design	Investment plans, insurance strategy
Tactical	Selection of medical protocols	Block planning, staffing, rostering	Supplier selection, tendering	Determining and allocating budgets, annual plans
Operational offline	Diagnosis and planning of an individual patient	Patient scheduling, workforce planning	Purchasing, determining order sizes	DRG billing
Operational online	Triage, diagnosing emergencies and complications	Monitoring, emergency coordination	Rush ordering	Billing complications

As indicated in the table, the operational offline planning level in the managerial area of resource capacity planning is the focus of this dissertation's scheduling problem. Scheduling decisions are performed by taking into account scarce resources. Therefore, the problem of the hospital-wide scheduling of patients addressed in this dissertation can be classified as a patient scheduling problem.

1.4 Topic of This Dissertation

Due to the DRG-reimbursement system described above which provides an incentive for hospitals to operate efficiently, the following factors will be taken into account in this dissertation: From the appointment request to the patient's admission, the way in which the patient's DRG can be more accurately predicted will be investigated. Then, assuming that the patient's DRG can be predicted reliably, a model formulation will be provided to take the information about DRGs into account to schedule the patient's treatments. In order to cope with uncertainty, a rolling horizon procedure will be developed.

More precisely, from a process perspective, as soon as an elective patient is referred by a general physician to the hospital, an appointment is negotiated for inpatient admission with the hospital's central bed management. Based on information regarding the patient's health condition, a working DRG should be calculated. By taking into account the availability of the patient and resource capacity, the admission date is fixed by the central bed manager and communicated to the patient. When the admission day comes, the patient is admitted to the ward in the respective specialty, and diagnostic treatments are performed. At this point in time, the working DRG will be recalculated based on the diagnostics findings. Afterwards, the surgery takes place, followed by recovery and, if necessary, rehabilitation, including physical therapy. After all necessary activities have been performed in the hospital, the patient is discharged and then, the final DRG is calculated.

This process reveals that the knowledge of the patient's DRG is essential during the entire care chain in order to make contribution margin-dependent scheduling decisions, e.g., when a patient is admitted to the hospital. Hence, as soon as the admission date is fixed and the patient arrives, it is necessary to decide which activity of the patient is scheduled when in order to reach the objective of maximizing contribution margin. The DRG is a homogeneous group of illnesses and severities which is linked to a revenue the hospital will receive from the patient's health insurance after the end of the treatment. As soon as the DRG of a patient is known, one can obtain average costs for the treatment of each patient type that is represented by DRG. Some of those costs are decision relevant and depend on LOS. Some costs, however, are not decision relevant because they belong to the medical treatment necessary for the patients recovery. At each point in time during the treatment, new information (e.g. further diagnoses) may become available which could influence the DRG. The more precisely the DRG can be predicted at any stage of care, the more accurately the contribution margin-dependent scheduling decisions can be made.

If one is able to know the patient's DRG at each point in time, further patient parameters may be determined in order to allocate resources more effectively and efficiently. Each patient has individual activities which have to be performed in a specific order where further temporal constraints have to be respected. These temporal orders can be understood as a clinical pathway, as mentioned in Sect. 1.2. Furthermore, resource requirement of activities as well as the resource capacity that is available to patients must be known. Moreover, the problem of uncertainty, which derives from at least two sources, has to be considered: Firstly, for each admitted patient uncertain recovery times have to be taken into account. Secondly, since emergency patients can arrive at any time, uncertainty exists about the remaining resource capacity for elective patients.

After having outlined the research problem, the following five research questions can be derived. Firstly, as soon as the patient contacts the hospital for admission, what information should be collected from the patient? Secondly, how can relevant attributes be connected in order to classify a patient into the correct DRG? Thirdly, as soon as the DRG can be predicted reliably, is it possible to formulate a model that maximizes contribution margin, based on scheduling decisions for a fixed admission date? Fourthly, relaxing the assumption of fixed admission dates, how can contribution margin be increased even further? Finally, does uncertainty in the recovery time and in the resources required by emergency patients have influence on the objective to maximize contribution margin?

These research questions will be answered in the following order. Firstly, the DRG grouping process will be evaluated before and at admission. Moreover, appropriate methods which are known from machine learning will be determined in order to select relevant attributes for the DRG classification process. Secondly, classification techniques that can be used to accurately classify DRGs will be studied. The third task is the formulation of a scheduling problem where the admission date is assumed to be fixed. Fourthly, the problem will be extended to the case when the admission date is flexible. Finally, a rolling horizon approach will be developed to analyze the influence of uncertainty on contribution margin.

1.5   Outline

The remainder of this dissertation is divided into four chapters. They are structured according to the chronological order of determining patient information first, followed by making scheduling decisions based on this information.

Chapter 2 reviews machine learning literature with a focus on health care. The chapter consists of an overview and a discussion of attribute selection approaches and classification techniques. The latter two are necessary to consider because on the one hand, hospital data is high dimensional and we are only interested in relevant and non-redundant predictors of DRG. On the other hand, DRG is a nominal attribute and therefore, the problem of assigning a patient to the correct DRG represents a classification problem. Next, attribute selection and classification methods that are used in the experimental study are described. Single classification techniques as well as a combination of these techniques will be evaluated. After relevant methods for classifying the DRG have been examined, scheduling models can be formulated that optimize the resource allocation based on DRGs. Chapter 3 starts with a literature review focusing on patient scheduling problems. Then, the fixed and the flexible admission date problems will be presented. Both are modeled as binary programs. Afterwards, the development of a rolling horizon approach is outlined in order to evaluate the influence of uncertainty on the economic improvement. Chapter 4 presents the experimental analysis of the current process in a collaborating hospital to determine a working DRG based on different assumptions for information available before and at admission. The performance of the machine learning approaches which are necessary for improving DRG classification accuracy will be analyzed in greater detail. The results from the attribute selection and classification approaches are reported and evaluated. Further, a computational study, an economic analysis and a length of stay analysis are provided for the static as well as the rolling horizon approaches. In this chapter, also the impact of uncertainty is evaluated when employing the rolling horizon approach. The concluding chapter contains a summary of the results including the main research contributions and suggestions for future research.

Chapter 2
Machine Learning for Early DRG Classification

In this chapter, a literature review of machine learning methods is provided with a special focus on attribute selection and classification methods successfully employed in health care. Similarities and differences between the machine learning methods addressed in this dissertation and the approaches available from the literature are highlighted. Afterwards, techniques for selecting relevant and non-redundant attributes for early DRG classification are presented. Finally, different classification techniques are described in detail.

2.1 Machine Learning for Health Care: A Literature Review

Attribute selection and classification are central methods of machine learning. Rather than employing large attribute sets for predicting or classifying a variable, it can be more efficient to select attributes in a first stage and afterwards to employ the selected attributes for prediction or classification. Textbook references for attribute selection and classification techniques are, among others, Bishop [22], Mackay [131] and Witten and Frank [233]. When considering attribute selection, Yu and Liu [239] divide the attribute selection process into three parts: Searching for irrelevant, weakly relevant and strongly relevant features, respectively. First, irrelevant features are not informative with respect to the class and can safely be ignored. Second, the set of weakly relevant features comprises redundant and non-redundant features. Third, strongly relevant features are always necessary for determining an optimal subset of features since removing a strongly relevant feature would necessarily affect the original conditional class distribution. The optimal subset of features is therefore the use of strongly relevant features and features that are weakly relevant but non-redundant.

After selecting an optimal set of features, a variable is predicted. The prediction process is denoted as a classification problem when the variable consists of different classes or categories. In the simplest case, the class variable is binary. However, it can consist of multiple features as well, as we will see in the case of early DRG

D. Gartner, *Optimizing Hospital-wide Patient Scheduling*, Lecture Notes in Economics and Mathematical Systems 674, DOI 10.1007/978-3-319-04066-0_2,
© Springer International Publishing Switzerland 2014

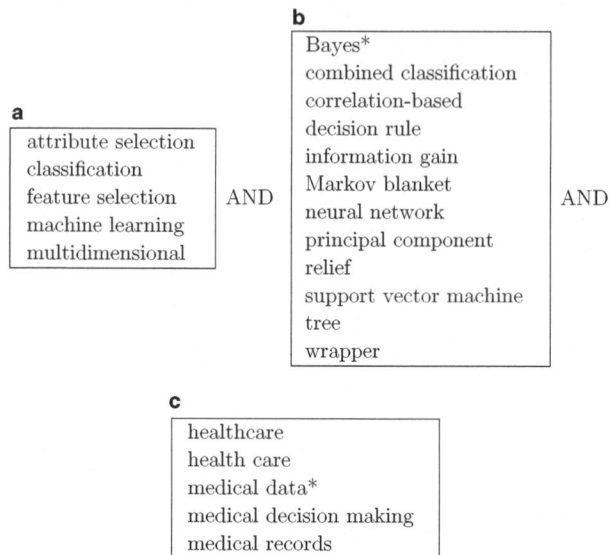

Fig. 2.1 Three-level structure of the search query including relevant tasks (**a**), machine learning methods (**b**) and field of research (**c**)

classification. In contrast, when predicting numeric or continuous attributes, those problems can be denoted as regression problems. In what follows, the focus is on classification problems.

2.1.1 Selection Criteria and Search for Relevant Literature

Attribute selection and classification methods are used in many health care applications and the following procedure describes a reproducible search for retrieving attribute selection and classification literature in the following fields: Health care, industrial engineering, medical informatics as well as operations research and the management sciences (OR/MS). English journal articles from the 2011 ISI journal citation report (JCR) science and social sciences edition (see [2]) were searched. Because of the aim to providing an interdisciplinary review, the subject categories anesthesiology, health policy and services, industrial engineering, medical informatics as well as OR/MS were selected within the JCR, yielding a total number of 206 relevant journals. Scopus (see [1]) was chosen as the search engine to retrieve the publications. The structure of the search query is presented in Fig. 2.1. The search string is divided hierarchically into (i) machine learning tasks (e.g., the selection of relevant attributes), (ii) machine learning methods (e.g. Markov blanket attribute selection) and (iii) field of research (e.g. health care). The asterisk (*) denotes a so-called "wildcard" which replaces character combinations of different length.

Table 2.1 Number of hits, irrelevant and remaining articles, categorized according to publication year

	1965–1997	1998–2002	2003–2007	2008–present	Total
#hits	32	55	87	154	328
#irrelevant articles	17	7	19	30	73
#remaining articles	15	48	68	124	255

For example, searching for "Bayes*" can result in, e.g., "Bayesian networks". Inside the boxes, the search strings are connected by an "OR" such that, e.g., articles that consider multiple machine learning methods can be retrieved. Moreover, the "ANDs" between the boxes ensure that the search space contains at least one keyword of each box. Note that the search does not exclude any strings by using "AND NOT", because false negative exclusions from the results should be avoided. However, exclusion criteria and the exclusion of irrelevant articles is described in the following section.

2.1.2 Classification of Relevant Literature

Table 2.1 presents summary statistics about the original 328 hits, excluded articles and the remaining 255 papers retrieved until May 22nd, 2013. An article is considered irrelevant if it focuses for example only on regression problems instead of classification problems (see, e.g., Bertsimas et al. [21]).

The table reveals that machine learning problems with a focus on health care are becoming increasingly popular in the literature and that in the last 5 years, more articles have been published than in any other of the previous time intervals. A forward search was performed, which means that more recent articles that cite the articles as given in Table 2.1 were included into the set of relevant papers. In addition, relevant contributions were discovered employing a backward search. This means that older articles that are cited within the references of the articles as given in Table 2.1 were reviewed and, if relevant, added to the set of relevant papers. In doing so, articles such as Hsieh et al. [88] and Kononenko et al. [107] were discovered using a forward and backward search, respectively. Within the set of relevant articles published since 1965, some literature reviews are available which are categorized in Table 2.2. The table shows that the set of journal articles contains nine literature reviews. Four of them focus on classification methods of which Harper [86] is the most recent. More specifically, Dreiseitl and Ohno-Machado [57] and Podgorelec et al. [166] limit their reviews to the methods neural networks and decision trees, respectively. However, the aim of this dissertations's review is, to provide an overview of different standard attribute ranking and selection as well as classification techniques. Another drawback of the existing literature reviews is that, for example, Scotch et al. [198] focus exclusively on biomedical

Table 2.2 Literature reviews on classification methods, decision support systems and statistical analyses in health care

	Publication year	Classification methods only	Decision support systems	Statistical analyses in general
Abad-Grau et al. [4]	2008		✓	
Dreiseitl and Ohno-Machado [57]	2002	✓		
Harper [86]	2005	✓		
Kononenko [107]	2001	✓		
Lee and Abbott [117]	2003			✓
Ohno-Machado [149]	2001			✓
Podgorelec et al. [167]	2002	✓		
Scotch et al. [198]	2010			✓
Smith et al. [207]	2003		✓	

informatics journals instead of providing a review for a broader audience. The aim of this dissertation's machine learning literature review is the discovery of relevant work in the field of, e.g., health care as well. Therefore, these nine reviews will be excluded from further examination. Moreover, only articles published since 2008 are categorized in order to give a picture of the recent developments in the interdisciplinary literature.

2.1.2.1 Attribute Ranking and Selection Techniques

Table 2.3 provides a categorization of the journal articles (from 2008–present) into different attribute ranking and selection technique categories. The table reveals that, the majority of the journal articles falls into the category "other attribute selection or evaluation techniques". One explanation for this is that in some of these articles, new attribute selection techniques are developed which are compared with standard techniques. Correspondingly, one can observe that a number of articles are represented in both, the category "other attribute selection or evaluation techniques" and in categories such as "information gain". Moreover, in some of these papers, the authors employ, e.g., regression models to discover relevant attributes. Alternatively or additionally, they decide based on expert opinions whether or not attributes are selected for the classification task. Besides this, many articles do not account for data preprocessing by selecting relevant attributes at all. Surprisingly, Markov blanket (MB) attribute selection was only discovered three times in the search for relevant publications although, it is a very useful hybrid approach for attribute selection and classification and is used in this dissertation to study attribute selection in connection with early DRG classification of inpatients.

Table 2.3 Overview of attribute ranking and selection methods employed in health care from 2008–present

Classification without attribute ranking/selection	[6, 7, 14, 17, 28, 39, 48, 50, 58, 72, 90, 97, 100, 109, 124, 129, 133, 139, 150, 164, 178, 187, 189– 192, 202, 208, 210, 211, 215, 217, 220, 230, 237, 240, 245]
Correlation-based	[5, 66, 71, 73, 88, 148]
Information gain	[5, 9, 16, 66, 68, 91, 94, 99, 104, 128, 148]
Markov blanket	[16, 88, 148]
Other attribute selection or evaluation techniques	[5, 9, 11, 12, 15, 19, 25, 37, 38, 40, 41, 47, 49, 52, 56, 59–61, 66– 68, 71, 73–75, 85, 88, 89, 94, 96, 98, 108, 110, 118, 122, 123, 128, 130, 132, 141–143, 146, 155–158, 168–170, 179, 180, 182, 183, 188, 209, 212, 221, 223, 225, 226, 232, 234–236, 241, 244, 246]
Principal component	[11, 119–121, 143, 213, 219]
Relief algorithms	[40, 41, 66, 148]
Wrapper	[40, 41, 43, 66, 71, 88, 91, 126, 127, 148, 153, 159, 161, 183, 214]

2.1.2.2   Classification Techniques

Table 2.4 provides a categorization of the journal articles into classification techniques. The table reveals that in most of the publications, support vector machines were employed, followed by other classification techniques and decision trees. On the contrary, decision rules as well as Bayesian networks, including Markov blanket represent the minority of the classification methods. Similar to the attribute selection techniques, the category "other classification techniques" contains, among others, innovative approaches that have been developed for specific classification tasks. One example for this is the work of Mu et al. [143] who employ principal component analysis as an attribute selection but employ discriminant analysis as a classification technique. Since the aim of this dissertation is to provide a general overview of standard methods, their application in health care and their evaluation for early DRG classification, the methods provided in the category "other classification techniques" are not examined in detail.

Among the articles, a number of publications deserve particular attention: Bai et al. [16], Fan and Chaovalitwongse [60] and Miettinen and Juhola [139]. These articles employ Bayesian models in order to pre-process data or to perform classification of medical diagnoses. Goodson and Jang [75] evaluate Bayesian networks in order to assess quality of care in the context of nursing home care.

Besides the articles classified above, further relevant publications are, e.g., Hall and Holmes [80] who study the connection between attribute selection and classification. They evaluate a sampling technique described by Robnik-Šikonja and Kononenko [184] and compare it with further attribute selection techniques using standard data sets. The attribute selection techniques are benchmarked

Table 2.4 Overview of classification methods employed in health care from 2008–present

Artificial neural networks	[11, 16, 19, 37, 43, 49, 50, 58, 73, 85, 88–90, 97, 99, 110, 118, 119, 121, 122, 124, 127, 129, 132, 133, 155, 169, 171, 209, 215, 219, 220, 223, 244]
Bayesian networks	[6, 16, 66, 75, 88, 122, 126, 133, 139, 150, 153, 210, 211, 246]
Combined classification	[6, 15, 28, 37, 39, 43, 52, 66, 74, 88, 89, 94, 97, 100, 109, 148, 153, 158, 171, 213, 220, 223, 226]
Decision rules	[6, 25, 52, 56, 61, 66, 91, 97, 99, 108, 123, 146, 148, 153, 158, 230, 232, 235]
Decision trees	[5, 6, 15, 17, 28, 37, 39, 43, 47–50, 66–68, 72, 74, 89–91, 94, 97, 99, 100, 104, 108, 109, 121, 122, 127, 129, 133, 153, 155, 157, 161, 168, 170, 171, 179, 180, 187, 189–192, 211, 214, 217, 226, 244, 246]
Markov blanket	[16, 88]
Naive Bayes	[6, 7, 12, 14, 16, 47, 48, 52, 59, 66, 68, 73, 74, 89, 97–99, 104, 109, 122, 124, 126, 132, 133, 139, 141, 148, 150, 153, 161, 182, 202, 211, 225, 230, 232]
Other classification techniques	[5, 6, 9, 16, 25, 38, 39, 43, 48, 60, 66–68, 71, 74, 75, 90, 91, 96–100, 104, 109, 110, 118, 121–124, 127, 129, 132, 133, 139, 141, 143, 153, 155, 158, 159, 161, 164, 168, 171, 178, 182, 183, 187–189, 212, 223, 225, 226, 234, 236]
Support vector machines	[5, 9, 16, 25, 39–41, 43, 47, 48, 50, 56, 60, 66, 68, 73, 88–90, 94, 97, 100, 109, 110, 120–122, 124, 128, 130, 132, 133, 141, 142, 148, 156, 158, 159, 164, 169, 178, 180, 182, 183, 187, 188, 190, 208, 212, 213, 221, 223, 234, 237, 240, 241, 244–246]

using two different classification methods. Methods that combine classification models are described by Kuncheva [111]. Similarly, in this dissertation, different attribute selection techniques that combine classifiers are evaluated. Ramiarina et al. [176] consider the prediction of a continuous attribute (costs) and thus employ a regression model. Similar to Bertsimas et al. [21] whose work was mentioned in the beginning (see Sect. 2.1.2), the study is excluded from the overview because the authors employ a regression model to predict health care costs. Instead, in this dissertation, a discrete attribute (DRG) is predicted and, therefore, we have a classification problem. Grubinger et al. [77] suggest the use of classification and regression trees in order to group inpatients with similar lengths of stay, instead of classifying individual patients. The results of their study are a selection of classification tree models and recommendations for the further development of the Austrian DRG system. Busse et al. [30] consider the problem of coding clinical data to the correct DRG from a quality management perspective. Coding quality highly influences classification and the assignment of the inpatient to the correct

DRG for billing purposes. However, Busse et al. [30] deal with the computation of DRGs after the discharge of the inpatient, whereas the problem addressed in this dissertation is to assign the inpatient to the appropriate DRG before and at admission for operations-driven DRG classification. In the next section, the methods employed for attribute selection and DRG classification are summarized.

2.2 Attribute Ranking and Selection Techniques Employed for Early DRG Classification

In what follows, a formal description of the early DRG classification problem is provided before the different approaches are presented. Let $\mathcal{I}$ denote a set of individuals (hospital inpatients) and let $\mathcal{D}$ denote the set of DRGs to which these individuals will be classified. For each inpatient $i \in \mathcal{I}$, we observe a set of attributes $\mathcal{A}$ at the time the patient contacts the hospital for admission, while the inpatient's true DRG, $d_i \in \mathcal{D}$, is computed once the inpatient is discharged. Let $\mathcal{V}_a$ denote the set of possible values for attribute $a \in \mathcal{A}$ and let $v_{i,a} \in \mathcal{V}_a$ denote the value of attribute a for inpatient i. As soon as inpatient i is admitted to the hospital, given the inpatient's values $v_{i,a}$ for each attribute $a \in \mathcal{A}$ the objective is to predict d_i. In this supervised learning problem, it is assumed that labeled training data from many other inpatients $j \in \mathcal{I} \setminus i$ is available in which attribute values $v_{j,a}$ and DRGs d_j are known. This training data is used to learn a classification model, which is then used for DRG prediction.

As indicated by the name, attribute ranking techniques provide an ordered list of attributes while attribute selection techniques select from all available attributes a subset of attributes which are relevant for classification. In this study, the following attribute selection techniques are considered: Information gain (IG), Relief-F attribute ranking (see Hall and Holmes [80]), Markov blanket attribute selection (see Bai et al. [16]), correlation-based feature selection (CFS) as well as wrapper attribute selection.

2.2.1 Information Gain Attribute Ranking

In order to describe the IG attribute ranking technique, the concept of information entropy is introduced. The idea is well-known from information theory and it measures the uncertainty associated with an attribute (see Sharma and Yu [205]). Given the prior probability $p(d)$ for each DRG $d \in \mathcal{D}$, the information entropy $H(\mathcal{D})$ is defined by Eq. (2.1).

$$H(\mathcal{D}) = -\sum_{d \in \mathcal{D}} p(d) \ln p(d) \tag{2.1}$$

Table 2.5 An example set of instances

i	d_i	$v_{i,1}$	$v_{i,2}$	$v_{i,3}$
1	I74C	Male	0–30	Fracture
2	I74C	Male	0–30	Fracture
3	I74C	Female	0–30	Fracture
4	I74C	Male	0–30	Chest pain
5	F62A	Male	0–30	Chest pain
6	F62A	Female	0–30	Pneumonia
7	F62A	Female	31–100	Pneumonia
8	F62A	Female	31–100	Pneumonia
9	F62A	Male	31–100	Pneumonia
10	F62A	Male	31–100	Heart failure
11	F62C	Female	31–100	Heart failure
12	F62C	Male	31–100	Heart failure

It holds for the discrete case and in the case that $p(d) = 0$, the convention is that $0 \ln(0) \equiv 0$ since $\lim_{x \to 0+} x \ln x = 0$ (see Mackay [131]). The negative sign ensures that $H(\mathcal{D})$ is positive or zero and the more uniform an attribute value is distributed over all instances, the higher is its entropy (see Bishop [22]). Using Eq. (2.2) one can compute the conditional information entropy $H(\mathcal{D}|a)$ of $\mathcal{D}$, given an attribute $a \in \mathcal{A}$. Here, $p(v)$ is the prior probability of attribute value $v \in \mathcal{V}_a$ for attribute $a \in \mathcal{A}$ and $p(d|v)$ is the conditional prior probability of a DRG d, given an attribute value $v \in \mathcal{V}_a$ of attribute $a \in \mathcal{A}$.

$$H(\mathcal{D}|a) = - \sum_{v \in \mathcal{V}_a} p(v) \sum_{d \in \mathcal{D}} p(d|v) \ln p(d|v) \qquad (2.2)$$

The information gain $IG(a)$ of each attribute $a \in \mathcal{A}$ is then computed by employing Eq. (2.3).

$$IG(a) = H(\mathcal{D}) - H(\mathcal{D}|a) \qquad (2.3)$$

The higher the information gain $IG(a)$ of an attribute $a \in \mathcal{A}$, the more valuable the attribute is assumed to be for classifying $\mathcal{D}$. In the following, the IG concept is illustrated using an example with the set of attributes $\mathcal{A} := \{gender, age, primary diagnosis\}$, the set of DRGs $\mathcal{D} := \{I74C, F62A, F62C\}$ as well as the sets of attribute values $\mathcal{V}_{gender} := \{male, female\}$, $\mathcal{V}_{age} := \{0–30, 31–100\}$ and $\mathcal{V}_{primary\ diagnosis} := \{fracture, chest pain, pneumonia, heart failure\}$. Twelve sample instances are provided by Table 2.5.

In this table, column $v_{i,1}$ contains the values of attribute "gender", $v_{i,2}$ the values of attribute "age" and $v_{i,3}$ the values of attribute "primary diagnosis". Summary statistics are provided by Table 2.6.

	I74C	F62A	F62C
Gender			
Male	3	3	1
Female	1	3	1
Age			
0–30	4	2	0
31–100	0	4	2
Primary diagnosis			
Fracture	3	0	0
Chest pain	1	1	0
Pneumonia	0	4	0
Heart failure	0	1	2
DRG			
	4	6	2

Table 2.6 Summary statistics of gender, age, primary diagnosis and DRG from the example provided by Table 2.5

Applying Eq. (2.1) to Table 2.6, the information entropy $H(\mathcal{D})$ of the class DRG $\mathcal{D}$ comes up to $H(\mathcal{D}) = -(\frac{4}{12} \ln \frac{4}{12} + \frac{6}{12} \ln \frac{6}{12} + \frac{2}{12} \ln \frac{2}{12}) = 1.011$. Using Eq. (2.2) and the conditional frequencies shown in Table 2.6, the conditional information entropy for the attribute "gender" can be computed as follows: $H(\mathcal{D}|\text{gender}) = -(\frac{7}{12}(\frac{3}{12} \ln \frac{3}{12} + \frac{3}{12} \ln \frac{3}{12} + \frac{1}{12} \ln \frac{1}{12}) + \frac{5}{12}(\frac{1}{12} \ln \frac{1}{12} + \frac{3}{12} \ln \frac{3}{12} + \frac{1}{12} \ln \frac{1}{12})) = 0.842$. Accordingly, the conditional entropies of the attributes "age" and "primary diagnosis" come up to $H(\mathcal{D}|\text{age}) = 0.664$ and $H(\mathcal{D}|\text{primary diagnosis}) = 0.404$. Using Eq. (2.3), the IG for the attribute "gender" is $IG(\text{gender}) = H(\mathcal{D}) - H(\mathcal{D}|\text{gender}) = 1.011 - 0.842 = 0.169$ and for "age" and "primary diagnosis", the information gains come up to $IG(\text{age}) = 0.347$ and $IG(\text{primary diagnosis}) = 0.607$, respectively. The results reveal that the attribute "primary diagnosis" has the highest IG, "age" has the second highest and "gender" has the lowest IG.

Since IG considers each attribute individually, and thus is ill-suited for examining the potential contribution of attribute combinations, the use of a further attribute ranking technique (Relief-F) will be examined.

2.2.2 Relief-F Attribute Ranking

Relief algorithms are known as fast feature selection algorithms (see Aliferis et al. [8]). Kira and Rendell [102] have developed this class of algorithms which has shown to be very efficient for binary classification problems (see Robnik-Šikonja and Kononenko [184]). The original algorithm has been refined by Robnik-Šikonja and Kononenko [184]: Their Relief-F variant is evaluated in this dissertation because, in contrast to Relief, it is not limited to two class problems and can deal with incomplete and noisy data (see Robnik-Šikonja and Kononenko [184]).

In order to describe the algorithm, the "k-nearest hits" and "k-nearest misses" for a sampled instance $i \in \mathcal{I}$ have to be defined. Let the set of k-nearest hits $\mathcal{H}_i(k) \subset \mathcal{I} \setminus i$ of an instance $i \in \mathcal{I}$ contain at most k instances $j \in \mathcal{I}, j \neq i$ which have the same DRG d_i as instance i. Specifically, those instances j are chosen with the same DRG such that $d_j = d_i$ and which have the lowest $diff_{i,j}$-values as defined by Eqs. (2.4) and (2.5).

$$diff_{i,j} = \sum_{a \in \mathcal{A}} diff_{i,j,a} \tag{2.4}$$

$$diff_{i,j,a} = \begin{cases} 0, & \text{if } v_{i,a} = v_{j,a} \\ 1, & \text{otherwise} \end{cases} \tag{2.5}$$

Furthermore, for each DRG $d \neq d_i$, let the set of k-nearest misses $\mathcal{M}_{d,i}(k) \subset \mathcal{I} \setminus i$ of instance i contain at most k instances $j \in \mathcal{I}, j \neq i$ with $d_j = d$ which have the lowest $diff_{i,j}$-values as defined by Eqs. (2.4) and (2.5). Both the k-nearest hits and the k-nearest misses for each DRG $d \in \mathcal{D}$ are inserted into Eq. (2.6) which computes the quality measure Q_a for attribute $a \in \mathcal{A}$.

$$Q_a = \frac{1}{k \cdot |\mathcal{I}|} \sum_{i \in \mathcal{I}} \left(- \sum_{h \in \mathcal{H}_i(k)} diff_{i,h,a} + \sum_{d \in \mathcal{D} \setminus d_i} \frac{p(d)}{1 - p(d_i)} \sum_{m \in \mathcal{M}_{d,i}(k)} diff_{i,m,a} \right) \tag{2.6}$$

For large data sets, this computation can be time-consuming. Therefore, an adaptation of this equation is provided which is employed in the Relief-F sampling algorithm while s denotes the number of samples. For attribute $a \in \mathcal{A}$ and a sampled instance $i \in \mathcal{I}$ the quality $Q_{a,i}$ is computed by Eq. (2.7), see Robnik-Šikonja and Kononenko [184].

$$Q_{a,i} = \frac{1}{k \cdot s} \left(- \sum_{h \in \mathcal{H}_i(k)} diff_{i,h,a} + \sum_{d \in \mathcal{D} \setminus d_i} \frac{p(d)}{1 - p(d_i)} \sum_{m \in \mathcal{M}_{d,i}(k)} diff_{i,m,a} \right) \tag{2.7}$$

Equation (2.7) is used in the sampling method, described by Algorithm 1. Here, $w(a)$ is a quality measure for each attribute $a \in \mathcal{A}$ updated in each iteration.

In what follows, the algorithm is illustrated with the example from Table 2.5 in which the user-defined parameters are set to $s = 5$ random samples and $k = 2$ "nearest-neighbors". Initially, the weights $w(a)$ are set for all attributes $a \in \mathcal{A}$ to 0 (see line 1). Afterwards, instance i is randomly selected from the data set (see line 3), e.g. instance $i = 3$ with DRG $d_3 = $ I74C. Computing the $diff_{3,j}$-values for all instances $j \in \mathcal{I} \setminus 3$ that have the same DRG as instance $i = 3$ leads to the following results: $diff_{3,1} = 1, diff_{3,2} = 1, diff_{3,4} = 2$. Thus, the set of the 2-nearest hits (see line 4) is $\mathcal{H}_3(2) = \{1, 2\}$. Accordingly, the sets of the 2-nearest misses (see line 6) $\mathcal{M}_{d,3}(2)$ are $\{5, 6\}$ and $\{11, 12\}$ for $d = $ F62A and $d = $ F62C, respectively. Now, for each attribute $a \in \mathcal{A}$ the attribute weight $w(a)$ is updated (see line 9).

Algorithm 1 Relief-F algorithm

Input parameters: k, s

Output parameters: $w(a) \quad \forall a \in \mathcal{A}$

1: $w(a) := 0 \quad \forall a \in \mathcal{A}$
2: **for** $l = 1$ to s **do**
3:      Randomly select an instance $i \in \mathcal{I}$
4:      $\mathcal{H}_i(k) := k$-nearest hits in $\mathcal{I}$ based on instance i
5:      **for all** $d \in \mathcal{D} \setminus d_i$ **do**
6:          $\mathcal{M}_{d,i}(k) := k$-nearest misses in $\mathcal{I}$ based on DRG d and instance i
7:      **end for**
8:      **for all** $a \in \mathcal{A}$ **do**
9:          $w(a) := w(a) + Q_{a,i}$
10:     **end for**
11: **end for**

Table 2.7 Sample-dependent sets and parameters as well as each attribute's current weight for each iteration of Relief-F

l	Sample-dependent sets and parameters							Attributes current weight		
	i	d_i	H_i	$M_{1,i}(2)$	$M_{2,i}(2)$	$Q_{1,i}$	$Q_{2,i}$	$Q_{3,i}$	$w(1)$	$w(2)$	$w(3)$
1	3	I74C	{1,2}	{5,6}	{11,12}	−0.100	0.050	0.200	−0.100	0.050	0.200
2	8	F62A	{7,9}	{3,4}	{11,12}	0.000	0.133	0.200	−0.100	0.183	0.400
3	12	F62C	{11}	{1,2}	{9,10}	−0.100	0.120	0.160	−0.200	0.303	0.560
4	7	F62A	{6,8}	{1,3}	{11,12}	0.100	0.033	0.200	−0.100	0.336	0.760
5	3	I74C	{1,2}	{5,6}	{11,12}	−0.100	0.050	0.200	−0.200	0.386	0.960

We start in iteration $l = 1$ and attribute $a = 1$ (gender). We compute the prior probabilities for the DRGs which are $p(d = \text{I74C}) = 0.333$, $p(d = \text{F62A}) = 0.500$ and $p(d = \text{F62C}) = 0.167$. Inserting these values into Eq. (2.6)

results in $Q_{1,3} = \frac{1}{2 \cdot 5}\left(-\sum_{h \in \mathcal{H}_3(2)} \text{diff}_{3,h,1} + \sum_{d \in \mathcal{D} \setminus d_3} \frac{p(d)}{1-p(d_3)} \sum_{m \in \mathcal{M}_{d,3}(2)} \text{diff}_{3,m,1}\right) =$

$\frac{1}{10} \cdot \left(-(1+1) + \frac{\frac{6}{12}}{1-\frac{4}{12}} \cdot (1+0) + \frac{\frac{2}{12}}{1-\frac{4}{12}} \cdot (0+1)\right) = -0.100$. Accordingly, $w(1) = -0.100$. The results of the example are provided in Table 2.7.

Table 2.7 reveals that instance $i = 3$ can be sampled twice from the set of instances. Robnik-Šikonja and Kononenko [184] do not specify whether sampling an instance more than once is allowed. The last row in Table 2.7 reveals that attribute 3 has the highest attribute weight and attribute 1 the lowest. This leads to the suggestion that attribute 3 (primary diagnosis) is the most relevant for classification.

So far two methods that basically compute a weight for each attribute with respect to the class $\mathcal{D}$ have been presented. The $IG(a)$ or $w(a)$ values of each attribute $a \in \mathcal{A}$ can be sorted by decreasing order (ranked). Then, the attributes with highest values can be selected for classification. As stated by Yu and Liu [239], a major drawback of the two methods presented so far is that they are not capable of detecting redundant attributes. This, however, can be overcome by using Markov blanket attribute selection, which will be introduced next.

Fig. 2.2 Markov blanket of
vertex $\mathcal{D}$

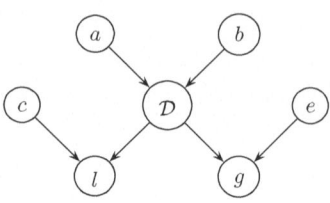

2.2.3   Markov Blanket Attribute Selection

In order to introduce Markov blanket attribute selection, the notation of Bayesian networks (BN), a type of probabilistic graphical model will be introduced. A Bayesian network is a directed acyclic graph (DAG) $\mathcal{G} := (\mathcal{V}, \mathcal{E})$ with vertices $\mathcal{V}$ and edges $\mathcal{E}$. In this graph, the vertices represent variables and the edges encode the conditional independence relationships between these variables (each variable is conditionally independent of its non-descendants in the graph given its parents). Pearl [160] and Wasserman [231] provide further theoretical properties of Bayesian networks and other probabilistic graphical models. For an overview of statistical graphical models with applications in systems biology, see Nagarajan et al. [144] as well as Scutari and Strimmer [200]. The Markov blanket of a vertex $v \in \mathcal{V}$, denoted by $MB(v)$, is a minimal subset of vertices containing vertex v, its direct parents and direct children as well as all direct parents of the children of v. The Markov blanket of vertex v contains all the variables needed to predict the value of that variable, since v is conditionally independent of all other variables given its Markov blanket. Figure 2.2 shows a sample Markov blanket DAG.

All vertices in the graph are part of the Markov blanket of vertex $\mathcal{D}$, since a and b are direct parents of $\mathcal{D}$, l and g are direct children of $\mathcal{D}$ and c and e are direct parents of the children of $\mathcal{D}$.

In this application of DRG classification, the vertices of the graph include the DRG variable ($\mathcal{D}$) as well as all attributes $a \in \mathcal{A}$. The aim is to select the subset of attributes which are relevant for predicting $\mathcal{D}$ and thus to be able to select those and only those variables in the Markov blanket of $\mathcal{D}$. Many methods have been developed to infer the Markov blanket of a variable from data, as described in Bai et al. [16] and Fu and Desmarais [69]. In order to describe the general procedure to derive a Markov blanket from data, the algorithm devised by Ramsey et al. [177] will be described because it can be illustrated straightforwardly with a simple example. With its breadth-first search strategy, the algorithm initially tries to connect all variables (many are similar, e.g. diagnoses) with the target variable DRG conditioned on a limited and therefore small subset of variables. The algorithm can be adapted for the discovery of the Markov blanket of a DRG as follows: The input parameters are the set of attributes $\mathcal{A}$, the set of DRGs $\mathcal{D}$ and a maximum search depth $d_{\max}$. The output is the Markov blanket of the target variable DRG, represented by the graph $\mathcal{G}$.

Algorithm 2 Markov blanket search heuristic

Input parameters: Set of attributes $\mathcal{A}$, set of DRGs $\mathcal{D}$, maximum search depth $d_{\max}$

Output parameter: Markov blanket $\mathcal{G} := (\mathcal{V}, \mathcal{E})$

1: $\mathcal{V} := \emptyset, \mathcal{E} := \emptyset, sepSet := \emptyset, Forbidden := \emptyset$
2: $\mathcal{V} := \mathcal{D} \cup \mathcal{A}$
3: $adj(\mathcal{D}) := checkedges(\mathcal{D})$
4: **for all** $a \in adj(\mathcal{D})$ **do**
5:     $adj(a) := checkedges(a)$
6: **end for**
7: **for all** $b \in adj(a) \setminus \{adj(\mathcal{D}) \cup \mathcal{D}\}$ **do**
8:     $adj(b) := checkedges(b)$
9: **end for**
10: $\mathcal{G} := orient\text{-}edges(\mathcal{G})$
11: $\mathcal{G} := trim\text{-}to\text{-}Markov\text{-}blanket(\mathcal{G})$

Algorithm 3 Checkedges (see Ramsey [177])

Input parameters: Vertex a, graph $\mathcal{G} := (\mathcal{V}, \mathcal{E})$, depth of search $d_{\max}$, set mapping $sepSet(a, b)$, set of edges $Forbidden$

Output parameters: Updated graph $\mathcal{G} := (\mathcal{V}, \mathcal{E})$, updated set mapping $sepSet(a, b)$, updated set of edges $Forbidden$

1: **for all** $b \in \mathcal{V} \setminus a$ **do**
2:     **if** $\{a, b\} \notin Forbidden$ **then** $\mathcal{E} := \mathcal{E} \cup \{a, b\}$
3:     **end if**
4: **end for**
5: **for** $depth = 0, \ldots, d_{\max}$ **do**
6:     **if** $|adj(a)| \geq depth + 1$ **then**
7:         **for all** $b \in adj(a)$ **do**
8:             **if** $b \amalg a|\mathcal{S}$ given $\mathcal{S} \subset \{adj(a) \setminus b\} : |\mathcal{S}| = depth$ **then**
9:                 $\mathcal{E} := \mathcal{E} \setminus \{a, b\}$
10:                $Forbidden \cup \{a, b\}$
11:                $sepSet\{a, b\} = \mathcal{S}$
12:            **end if**
13:        **end for**
14:    **end if**
15: **end for**

Here, $adj(a)$ denotes the set of adjacent vertices of the vertex a. For testing conditional independence, the χ^2-test can be used with an $\alpha = 5\%$ level of significance. The result of this test $(a \amalg b|\mathcal{A})$ denotes that attribute $a \in \mathcal{A}$ is conditionally independent of attribute $b \in \mathcal{A} \setminus a$ given further attributes $\mathcal{A}$: $a, b \notin \mathcal{A}$. The set of unordered pairs $\{a, b\} \in Forbidden$ denotes forbidden edges in the graph, determined by the function *checkedges* which is described by Algorithm 3.

An edge is forbidden if a subset of attributes $\mathcal{S} \subset \mathcal{V} \setminus \{a, b\}$ exists that separates a from b. For each edge $\{a, b\} \in Forbidden$ a set mapping $sepSet(a, b) = \mathcal{S}$ exists which in turn contains $\mathcal{S}$. $sepSet(a, b)$ and $Forbidden$ are updated synchronously

Algorithm 4 Orient-edges (see Ramsey [177]). For the definition of a collider, see
e.g. Wasserman [231]. The asterisk (*) can be the head or the tail of an arc such that
e.g. $a * -b$ can denote (b, a) or $\{a, b\}$
Input parameter: $\mathcal{G} := (\mathcal{V}, \mathcal{E})$
Output parameter: $\mathcal{G} := (\mathcal{V}, \mathcal{E})$

```
 1: for all triples of vertices {a, b, c} ∈ V do
 2:     if a * −b − *c, a ∉ adj(c), b ∉ sepSet(a, c) then orient a* → b ← *c.
 3:     end if
 4: end for
 5: for all 4-tuples of vertices {a, b, c, d} ∈ V do
 6:     if a → b, b − c, a ∉ adj(c), ¬(a → b ← c) then b → c.
 7:     end if
 8:     if a → b, b → c, a − c then a → c.
 9:     end if
10:     if a − b, a − c, a − d, c → b, d → b then a → b.
11:     end if
12:     if a − b, b ∈ adj(d), a ∈ adj(c), a − d, b → c, c → d then a → d.
13:     end if
14: end for
```

by *checkedges* where $adj(a)$ denotes the set of adjacent vertices of the vertex a.
Orient-edges orients edges to arcs and is presented in Algorithm 4.

After the initialization in line 1, the algorithm sets the set of vertices equal to
DRG and the set of attributes. *checkedges* adds for all attributes $a \in \mathcal{A}$ an edge from
a to $\mathcal{D}$ such that $\mathcal{E} := \mathcal{E} \cup \{a, \mathcal{D}\}$. Next, the algorithm tests, conditioned on subsets
of the vertices in the graph, whether or not an edge $\{a, \mathcal{D}\}$ can be removed from $\mathcal{E}$.
An edge $\{a, \mathcal{D}\}$ is removed if there is a subset $\mathcal{S} \subset \mathcal{V} \backslash \{a, \mathcal{D}\}$ of vertices in the graph
such that $(a \amalg \mathcal{D}|\mathcal{S})$. Here, $|\mathcal{S}|$ is limited by the user-defined parameter d_{max}, which
is the maximum search depth. Depending on d_{max} and the speed of the conditional
independence test, this procedure can be time-consuming. Next, the same procedure
is performed with adjacents of $\mathcal{D}$ and adjacents of the adjacents of $\mathcal{D}$. Note that
until line 9 in Algorithm 2, we search an undirected graph. After that, Algorithm 4
orients the edges to arcs and different orientation rules are applied while ensuring
that the property of acyclicity is retained (see Meek [137] and Bai et al. [16]) until
no further orientation can be made. Finally, when reaching line 11 of Algorithm 2
the graph $\mathcal{G}$ is trimmed to the Markov blanket of $\mathcal{D}$ so that a Markov blanket DAG
is returned.

In what follows, an example is provided by employing the publicly available data
set "learning.test" containing discrete attributes (see Scutari [199]). It consists of the
set of attributes $\mathcal{A} = \{A, \ldots, F\}$. The causal network including the Markov blanket
of attribute A is provided in Fig. 2.3.

Assume, the Markov blanket of the attribute A has to be inferred. Let the results
of the conditional independence tests during the execution of *checkedges* be: $(C \amalg A|\emptyset), (F \amalg A|\emptyset), (E \amalg A|B), (C \amalg B|\emptyset), (F \amalg B|\emptyset), (D \amalg B|A), (F \amalg D|\emptyset), (E \amalg D|A), (C \amalg E|\emptyset), (F \amalg C|\emptyset)$. Figure 2.4 shows the different steps of the algorithm

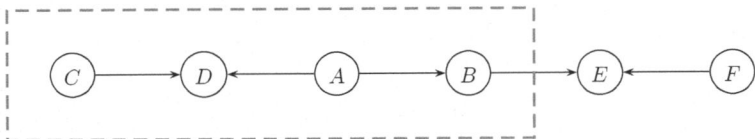

Fig. 2.3 Causal network of the example (see Scutari [199]) including the Markov blanket of attribute *A* (*dashed gray rectangle*)

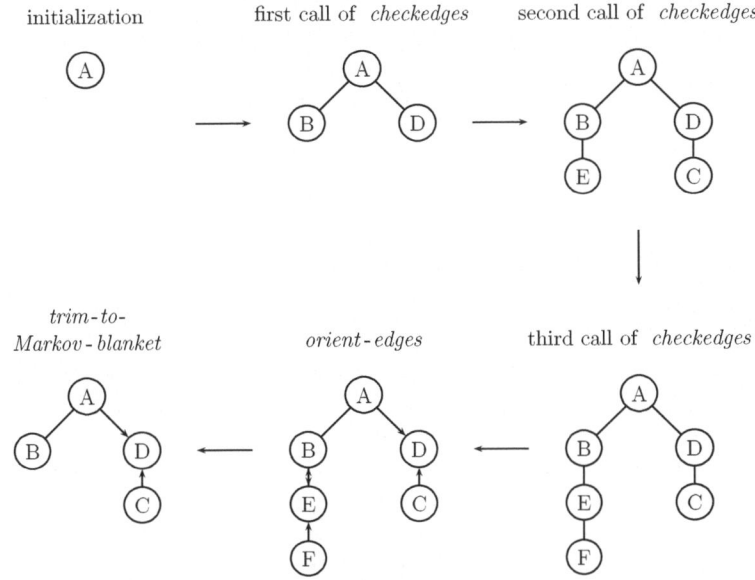

Fig. 2.4 Different steps during the Markov blanket search

when using $d_{\max} = 1$, the χ^2-test as used by Scutari [199] and a confidence level of $\alpha = 5\,\%$. Table 2.8 shows the sets after the termination of the algorithm.

Note that in the *orient-edges*-step, the edge $\{A, B\}$ cannot be oriented since *B* is an element of the set that separates *A* from *E* (see line 2 of Algorithm 4). Because of the Markov condition in undirected graphs (see Wasserman [231]), *B* separates *E* and *F* from *A* such that the Markov blanket of *A* is $MB(A) = \{A, B, C, D\}$ which is correct (cf. Fig. 2.3).

Besides Ramsey's [177] algorithm, many other methods have been developed to obtain the Markov blanket of a variable from data. In this dissertation, two of them will be evaluated: The so-called Grow-Shrink approach (GS) devised by Margaritis [135] and the Incremental-Association search (IA) devised by Tsamardinos et al. [218]. The reason to employ these algorithms is because arcs can be fixed in the Markov blanket DAG of which a functional relationship between attributes and DRG are known as required by the DRG system (see Fig. 1.1). Hence, it can be controlled that these attributes are not considered irrelevant or redundant.

Set	Elements
Table 2.8 Sets after the third call of the *checkedges* algorithm to find adjacents of the adjacents of the vertex A	
$\mathcal{V}$	A, B, C, D, E, F
$\mathcal{E}$	$\{A, B\}, \{A, D\}, \{E, B\}, \{C, D\}, \{F, E\}$
$Forbidden$	$\{A, C\}, \{A, F\}, \{A, E\}, \{B, D\}, \{B, C\},$ $\{B, F\}, \{F, D\}, \{E, D\}, \{C, E\}, \{C, F\}$
$sepSet(A, C)$	$\emptyset$
$sepSet(A, F)$	$\emptyset$
$sepSet(A, E)$	B
$sepSet(B, D)$	A
$sepSet(B, C)$	$\emptyset$
$sepSet(B, F)$	$\emptyset$
$sepSet(F, D)$	$\emptyset$
$sepSet(E, D)$	A
$sepSet(C, E)$	$\emptyset$
$sepSet(C, F)$	$\emptyset$

2.2.4 Correlation-Based Feature Selection

Another way to select attributes is to select ones that individually correlate well with the class (DRG) and have low intercorrelation with other individual attributes. In order to compute the intercorrelation of two nominal attributes a and b, nominal attributes are the majority of attributes evaluated in this dissertation (see Table B.1), one has to compute the symmetrical uncertainty $U(a, b) \in [0; 1]$ by employing the following equation (see, e.g., Hall and Holmes [80]):

$$U(a, b) = 2 \cdot \frac{H(a) + H(b) - H(a|b)}{H(a) + H(b)}. \tag{2.8}$$

Again, $H(a)$ is the entropy of attribute a (see Eq. (2.1)) while $H(a|b)$ is the conditional entropy of attribute a given attribute b using Eq. (2.2). The attribute subset $\mathcal{A}_i^*$ which maximizes the following expression is selected:

$$\mathcal{A}_i^* = \arg \max_{\mathcal{A}' \subset \mathcal{A}} \frac{\sum\limits_{a \in \mathcal{A}'} U(a, \mathcal{D})}{\sqrt{\sum\limits_{a \in \mathcal{A}'} \sum\limits_{b \in \mathcal{A}' \setminus a} U(a, b)}}. \tag{2.9}$$

2.2.5 Wrapper Attribute Selection

In what follows, a method will be described that "wraps" a classification scheme into the attribute selection procedure. For this attribute subset evaluation, a classification scheme as well as an evaluation measure have to be chosen that will be optimized, e.g. accuracy (Acc.). The approach is described in Table 2.9 using $\mathcal{A} := \{a, b, c\}$ as a set of attributes (for details, see Kohavi and John [105]).

Table 2.9 Wrapper attribute subset evaluation in order to produce a ranked list of attributes

Iteration 1			Iteration 2			Iteration 3		
Attribute set	Acc.	Best attribute	Attribute set	Acc.	Best attribute	Attribute set	Acc.	Best attribute
a	0.1		*a* *b*	0.3		*a* *b* *c*	0.35	
b	**0.3**	*b*	*b* *c*	**0.4**	*c*	*b* *c*	**0.4**	–
c	0.2							

Starting with an empty subset of attributes, in each iteration one (best) single attribute is added to the list of attributes. In the example, we choose in the first iteration attribute *b* since it has the highest gain in accuracy (see Table 2.9). In the second iteration (see Table 2.9) we check whether attribute *a* or *c* can improve classification accuracy. Since the additional attribute *c* results in the highest increase of accuracy, it is added to the set of attributes. Finally, based on attributes *b* and *c* during the third iteration (see Table 2.9) accuracy is evaluated again to check whether attribute *a* can improve accuracy. Since accuracy cannot be improved, the subset $\{b, c\} \subset \mathcal{A}$ is selected as the best subset of attributes. Usually, this greedy search goes along with high computational effort which depends on the complexity of the classification scheme and on the number of attributes, among others.

2.3 Classification Techniques Employed for Early DRG Classification

In the following, six classification methods will be summarized: Naive Bayes (NB), Bayesian networks (BN), classification trees (also called decision trees), a method that combines these classifiers by voting, a probability averaging approach (PA) and a straightforward decision rule. For each method, the classifier is learned from a dataset of labeled training examples. This means that the true DRG of each inpatient is known to the classification method. Afterwards, the classifier is applied to a separate dataset of unlabeled test examples. Here, the true DRG of each inpatient is unknown to the classification method and must be predicted. The naive Bayes and Bayesian network methods infer a probabilistic model from the training data and compute the posterior probability that the inpatient belongs to a DRG *d* given the inpatient's attributes $\mathcal{A}$. Then, the inpatient is assigned to that DRG with the highest posterior probability. The classification tree method, instead, infers a tree-structured set of decision rules from the training data and uses these rules to predict the inpatient's DRG. The voting and the probability averaging approaches assign the patient to that DRG which receives the highest support based on the individual classification methods. Finally, a decision-rule based approach is presented, based on historical data. In the following, each method will be described in more detail.

2.3.1 Naive Bayes

The naive Bayes classifier assumes that all of an inpatient's attributes $a \in \mathcal{A}$ are conditionally independent, given the inpatient's DRG d. Under this assumption, the classifier assigns the DRG d_i^* to the test instance i employing Eq. (2.10).

$$d_i^* = \arg\max_{d \in \mathcal{D}} \left\{ p(d) \prod_{a=1}^{|\mathcal{A}|} p(v_{i,a}|d) \right\} \tag{2.10}$$

The prior probability $p(d)$ of each DRG d is learned from the training data by maximum likelihood estimation, i.e., $p(d)$ is set equal to the proportion of training examples which belong to class d. Similarly, the conditional likelihood of each attribute value $v_{i,a}$ given each DRG d is learned from the training data by maximum likelihood estimation, i.e., $p(v_{i,a}|d)$ is set equal to the proportion of training examples of class d which have value $v_{i,a}$ for attribute a.

In what follows, data from Table 2.5 is employed to provide an example for the naive Bayes classification. The data set is split into one test instance (instance 1) and 10 training instances (instances 2–11). The prior probabilities for each DRG in the training set are $p(\text{I74C}) = 0.273$, $p(\text{F62A}) = 0.545$ and $p(\text{F62C}) = 0.182$. Employing Eq. (2.10) the conditional probability for predicting the DRG of instance $i = 1$ and $d = \text{I74C}$ is $p(\text{I74C}) \cdot p(\text{male}|\text{I74C}) \cdot p(0\text{–}30|\text{I74C}) \cdot p(\text{fracture}|\text{I74C}) = 0.273 \cdot 0.182 \cdot 0.273 \cdot 0.182 = 0.002$. This is the maximum conditional probability for all DRGs $d \in \mathcal{D}$ so that the DRG of instance $i = 1$ is classified to $d_1^* = \text{I74C}$ which is correct.

This way of computing conditional probabilities is ill-suited to predicting the DRG, when events have not yet been observed. In the case of Tables 2.5 and 2.6, for example, the conditional probability of $p(\text{F62C}|0\text{–}30) = 0$. Accordingly, for Eq. (2.10), with any DRG d of which its conditional attribute value $v_{i,a}$ has not been observed, the entire conditional probability would become zero. To overcome this problem of underestimation, a Laplace estimator is commonly employed by simply adding 1 to each count (see Witten and Frank [233]).

2.3.2 Bayesian Networks

The naive Bayes approach assumes that each attribute is only dependent on the DRG but not dependent on other attributes, which is rarely true. Thus, the naive Bayes classifier is extended to a Bayesian network classifier, in which the set of conditional independence assumptions is encoded in a Bayesian network as described above. As in the naive Bayes approach, conditional probabilities are inferred from the training data, but now we must condition not only on the DRG d, but also on any other parents Π_a of the given attribute a in the Markov blanket graphical model:

$$d_i^* = \arg\max_{d \in \mathcal{D}} \left\{ p(d) \prod_{a=1}^{|\mathcal{A}|} p(v_{i,a} | d, \Pi_a) \right\} \qquad (2.11)$$

Similar to the naive Bayes approach, the instance is assigned to that DRG d_i^* which has the highest posterior probability, as in the naive Bayes approach.

Given the graph in Fig. 2.2 an estimator of the conditional probabilities can be obtained by computing conditional probabilities of the vertices in the Markov blanket. Let us assume that the set of DRGs consists of d_1 and d_2. Further, assume that an instance $i = 1$ with attribute values $v_{1,a}, v_{1,b}, v_{1,c}, v_{1,e}, v_{1,l}, v_{1,g}$ has to be classified. We also assume that we have test instances that have been used to compute the necessary conditional probabilities that can be derived from the graph. To classify the instance, we compute $p(\mathcal{D} = d_1 | v_{1,a}, v_{1,b}, v_{1,c}, v_{1,e}, v_{1,l}, v_{1,g}) = p(a = v_{1,a} | d_1) \cdot p(b = v_{1,b} | d_1) \cdot p(l = v_{1,l}, c = v_{1,c} | d_1) \cdot p(g = v_{1,g}, e = v_{1,e} | d_1)$ and $p(\mathcal{D} = d_2 | v_{1,a}, v_{1,b}, v_{1,c}, v_{1,e}, v_{1,l}, v_{1,g}) = p(a = v_{1,a} | d_2) \cdot p(b = v_{1,b} | d_2) \cdot p(l = v_{1,l}, c = v_{1,c} | d_2) \cdot p(g = v_{1,g}, e = v_{1,e} | d_2)$. Finally, the instance is assigned to that DRG which has the highest probability. As for naive Bayes, for attribute values in the test instance that have not yet occurred in the set of training instances, the conditional probability would be zero. In this case, a nearest-neighbor heuristic (see e.g. Bai et al. [16]) can be used.

2.3.3 Classification Trees

As stated in Sect. 1.1, the hospital where this study was undertaken employs a DRG grouper to determine the DRG of an inpatient from the second day after admission. The algorithm which is implemented in this software is similar to a classification tree: It is a tree-structured set of rules which deterministically computes each inpatient's DRG given their attribute values. In the context of this dissertation, a classification tree is a hierarchical data structure that consists of a root node which represents an attribute. Additional nodes that represent further attributes, except the "root attribute", are linked with the root node directly or indirectly. Leaf nodes represent the DRGs. Arcs between nodes represent the values of the attributes located in the predecessor hierarchy. A sample classification tree is shown in Fig. 2.5.

Instead of using a pre-existing set of decision rules as employed by the DRG grouper, we learn the classification tree automatically from the labeled training dataset. There are various methods to learn the structure of a classification tree from data: In this dissertation, Quinlan's algorithm [175] will be evaluated which has also been investigated by Hall and Holmes [80] with respect to attribute selection. The advantage of employing this approach is that the over-fitting of the classification tree as well as the tree size during the learning process can be controlled.

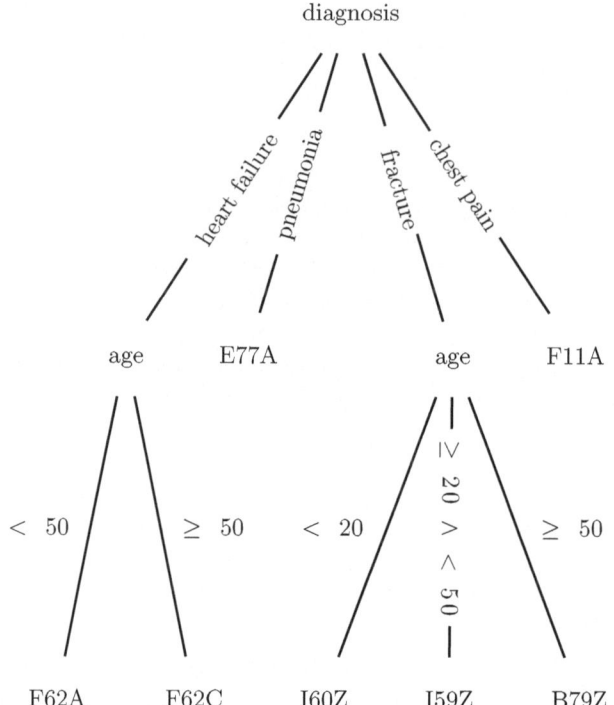

Fig. 2.5 Sample classification tree

The algorithm works as follows: In the first step, the attribute a^* with the maximum information gain is selected from the set of attributes $\mathcal{A}$. Based on a^*, which becomes the root node, $\mathcal{I}$ is divided into subsets $\mathcal{I}_v$; each one contains different values $v \in \mathcal{V}_{a^*}$ of attribute a^*. Each value is represented by an edge. If in any subset $\mathcal{I}_v$ only one DRG d exists, the attribute value v is assigned directly to that DRG. Otherwise, the attribute with the next highest IG is selected from the attribute set and linked to those DRGs by an edge. It is split recursively, further on each subset of attribute values.

In the following, the method is illustrated based on the example in Table 2.5. For the sake of simplicity, instances 1–10 are considered. Table 2.10 provides the summary statistics of instances 1–10 for which the information entropy can be computed.

Using Eq. (2.1), the information entropy for the class attribute $\mathcal{D}$ comes up to $H(\mathcal{D}) = 0.673$ while the conditional entropies for "gender", "age" and "primary diagnosis" are $H(\mathcal{D}|\text{gender}) = 0.670$, $H(\mathcal{D}|\text{age}) = 0.600$ and $H(\mathcal{D}|\text{primary diagnosis}) = 0.370$, respectively. Using Eq. (2.3), the IG for the attribute "gender" is $IG(\text{gender}) = 0.003$ and for "age" and "primary diagnosis", the information gains come up to $IG(\text{age}) = 0.073$ and $IG(\text{primary diagnosis}) = 0.303$, respectively. The results reveal that the attribute "primary diagnosis" has the highest IG and as

Table 2.10 Summary statistics of gender, age, primary diagnosis and DRG for instances 1–10 from the example provided by Table 2.5

	I74C	F62A
Gender		
Male	3	3
Female	1	3
Age		
0–30	4	2
31–100	0	4
Primary diagnosis		
Fracture	3	0
Chest pain	1	1
Pneumonia	0	4
Heart failure	0	1
DRG		
	4	6

Fig. 2.6 Selected part of the classification tree before the addition of further nodes

primary diagnosis

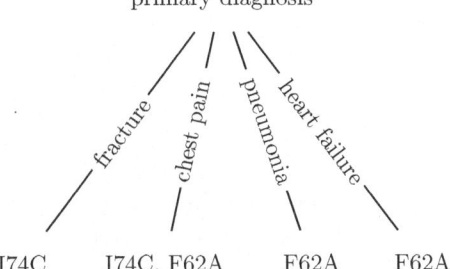

a result, the decision tree grows by selecting this attribute as the root node, see Fig. 2.6.

Since the attribute values "fracture", "pneumonia" and "heart failure" cannot be split further, the class is directly assigned to the respective attribute value. However, instances that contain the attribute value "chest pain" can be differentiated because here, the classes $d = $ I74C and $d = $ F62A occur. Thus, the instances are split by choosing between the remaining attributes "gender" and "age". Both have an IG of 0 from Table 2.5 one can observe that instances in which "chest pain" occurred ($i = $ 4, 5), the attribute values for "gender" and "age" are not different, conditioned on the class DRG. Therefore, we randomly assign the attribute "gender" to the attribute value "chest pain" which contains $d = $ I74C and $d = $ F62A. Now, we have to split on "age". The IG for this last attribute is, again, 0 such that we randomly select class $d = $ I74C to the attribute value "0–30" which is illustrated by Fig. 2.7. The decision tree growing process usually results in an unnecessarily large and highly specific structure. Thus, methods should be considered in order to prune the decision tree. In this dissertation, the C4.5 pruning strategy (see Witten and Frank [233]) will be evaluated. Firstly, we determine for each node the subset of training instances that is represented by the node. Secondly, we identify the DRG

Fig. 2.7 Final classification
tree

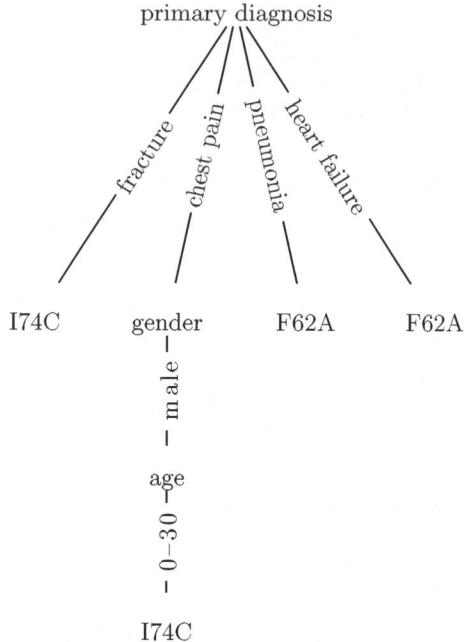

that represents the majority of instances reaching the node. Thirdly, an error rate
which is the number of instances not represented by this DRG is calculated.
Fourthly, by specifying a confidence level (see Sect. 4.1.6 for an evaluation of
different confidence levels), we calculate the node's upper error bound. Finally, we
compare this bound with its children's error rates. If the children's combined error
rates are greater than the bound, the children are pruned away from the node and
replaced by a leaf.

2.3.4   Voting-Based Combined Classification

Another classification approach is to combine classifiers in order to take advantage
of each individual classifier's strengths. Different methods to combine classifiers in
order to increase classification accuracy are described in Kittler et al. [103] and the
following method is used in the context of this dissertation. Given the input vector
of attribute values for an instance, for each DRG we count the number of classifiers
which lead to the selection of this DRG. The DRG which receives the largest number
of votes is then chosen while ties are resolved by employing a uniform random
distribution.

2.3.5   Probability Averaging to Combine the DRG Grouper with Machine Learning Approaches

The following new approach has been developed in this dissertation in order to combine a DRG grouper with machine learning based classification approaches. The DRG grouper is employed as a classifier and combined with the decision tree and the Bayesian network approach. Given the probability of DRG d for classifier c as $p_{c,d}$, a new instance i is classified by employing the following rule:

$$d_i^* = \arg\max_{d \in \mathcal{D}} \frac{1}{|\mathcal{C}|} \cdot \sum_{c \in \mathcal{C}} p_{c,d}. \tag{2.12}$$

Naturally, for the two classifiers DRG grouper and decision tree, the probability for DRG d and classifier c is $p_{c,d} \in \{0, 1\}$. In contrast, in the probability distribution of the third approach, i.e. the Bayesian network classifier, the probability distribution is $p_{c,d} \in [0, 1]$. Accordingly, if the first two classifiers (DRG grouper and classification trees) support two different DRGs $d = 1$ and $d = 2$, and the Bayesian network has strong but not maximum support for a third DRG $d = 3$, i.e., $p_{3,3} \neq 100\%$ then the third DRG becomes irrelevant and the tie-breaker for choosing d_i^* is the DRG with the higher probability based on the Bayesian network's probability distribution. Then, if the probabilities for the two remaining DRGs are equal, ties are resolved by employing a uniform random distribution.

2.3.6   Decision Rule-Based Mapping of Attribute Values to DRGs

Holte [87] examines the performance of simple decision rules where attribute values are mapped directly to class values. For the problem of early DRG classification, the rules are determined as follows: In the training set, we count how often an attribute value of "admission diagnosis 1" occurred with respect to each DRG. For each attribute value, a mapping to the most frequent DRG is created. If two DRGs have the same frequency for the same "admission diagnosis 1", the DRG is assigned which appeared first in the training set. The default DRG is the one with the highest frequency in the entire training set. Now, for each instance in the testing set, the value of "admission diagnosis 1" is observed and the instance to the DRG which is described by the decision rule is assigned. If the "admission diagnosis 1" has not yet been observed in the training set, the default DRG is assigned.

Chapter 3
Scheduling the Hospital-Wide Flow of Elective Patients

The structure of this chapter is as follows: Firstly, a literature review on patient scheduling and capacity allocation problems in health care is provided. Similarities and differences between the scheduling problems addressed in this dissertation and the approaches available from the literature are highlighted. Secondly, the patient flow problem with fixed admission dates is presented. Thirdly, the patient flow problem with variable admission dates is described, followed by an example for both the fixed and variable admission date problem. Both problems have been published by Gartner and Kolisch [70] who apply, in addition, a rolling horizon approach which is presented for scheduling the hospital-wide flow of elective patients in Sect. 3.5.

3.1 Mathematical Programming Applied to Patient Scheduling in Hospitals: A Literature Review

There is a large amount of literature available that covers capacity allocation problems in health care. Textbooks are, among others, Brandeau et al. [27], Hall [81, 82], Kolker [106], Langabeer [116], Ozcan [151, 152], Shiver and Eitel [206], Vissers and Beech [229] and Yih [238]. Hulshof et al. [92] provide a valuable taxonomic classification of planning decisions in health care for the OR/MS community. Focusing on hospitals, Vanberkel et al. [222] provide a literature review on the planning of multiple hospital departments while Cardoen et al. [34] and Guerriero and Guido [78] offer ones on planning the operating theater. In the following subsections, a literature review will be provided that focuses on mathematical programming approaches successfully applied to patient scheduling in hospitals. Selection criteria will be defined in order to identify journal articles which will be categorized into different health care services, resources considered, modelling and solution approaches, modelling and evaluation of risk as well as patient and resource related objectives. One motivation to provide a different literature review

D. Gartner, *Optimizing Hospital-wide Patient Scheduling*, Lecture Notes in Economics
and Mathematical Systems 674, DOI 10.1007/978-3-319-04066-0_3,
© Springer International Publishing Switzerland 2014

Table 3.1 Number of articles in the original result set, categorized according to publication year

	2000–2004	2005–2009	2010–present	Total
#articles	5	15	22	42

as compared to the existing ones is because this classification shall close the gap between Hulshof et al.'s [92] broad and exhaustive review on planning problems in health care and Cardoen et al.'s [34] detailed classification of operating room (OR) planning problems.

3.1.1 Selection Criteria and Search for Relevant Literature

Since the patient scheduling problem addressed in this dissertation is located on the operational offline planning level (see Table 1.2), the patient scheduling problems within the health care services "ambulatory care services", "inpatient care services", "surgical care services" and "residential care services" (see Hulshof et al. [92]) are examined in more detail. Moreover, since in this dissertation mathematical programming is employed to schedule the hospital-wide flow of elective patients, articles are limited to mathematical programming and exclude staff-to-shift assignment. All papers that match these criteria are extracted from Hulshof et al.'s [92] literature review and considered as base set of articles. This set is extended by improving Hulshof et al.'s [92] search query. For example, the term "inpatient*" was added to the search query that focuses on "inpatient care services". Moreover, missing publications such as Hanne et al. [83], Ogulata and Erol [147] and Ozkarahan [154] as well as recent publications that were retrieved until May 22nd, 2013 such as Vijayakumar et al. [227] are included in this review.

3.1.2 Classification of Relevant Literature

Employing these selection criteria, a total number of 42 papers were retrieved and are considered relevant for this dissertation. The articles can be categorized in publication years as given in Table 3.1.

The table reveals that this field of research is becoming increasingly popular since the number of publications from 2010–present is more than four times higher than the one between 2000–2004. In the next subsections, a classification framework for these articles will be provided, breaking down these papers into health care services, resources, modelling and solution approaches, consideration of risk and objectives.

Table 3.2 Health care services

Ambulatory care services	
Appointment series scheduling	[18, 44–46]
Single appointment scheduling	[174]
Inpatient care services	
Admission scheduling	[35, 46, 51]
Transportation scheduling	[83]
Surgical care services	
Surgical case scheduling	[13, 20, 31–33, 36, 42, 53–55, 62– 65, 79, 95, 113–115, 134, 136, 138, 140, 147, 154, 163, 165, 181, 186, 216, 227]
Residential care services	
Treatment scheduling	[76, 193, 203]

Table 3.3 Aggregate overview of single vs. multiple resources considered

Single resources	[18, 35, 44, 45, 51, 54, 55, 76, 113– 115, 134, 174]
Multiple (different) resources	[13, 20, 31–33, 36, 42, 46, 53, 62– 65, 79, 83, 95, 136, 138, 140, 147, 154, 163, 165, 181, 186, 193, 203, 216, 227]

3.1.2.1   Health Care Services

Table 3.2 shows the classification of the articles with respect to the different types of health care services, following the classification of Hulshof et al. [92]. Note that home care planning is not considered explicitly in this review since this dissertation focuses exclusively on hospitals. However, the article of Bard and Shao [18] that focuses primarily on home care is included because their work is located on the interface between home care and hospitals where therapists can be scheduled for patient treatments in a hospital. The table reveals that the majority of the articles focuses on surgical care services while treatment scheduling for example in rehabilitation hospitals (see Schimmelpfeng et al. [193]) is considered rarely in the literature. Note that Conforti et al. [46] can be categorized into both ambulatory and inpatient care services because their week-hospital approach which is described later in greater detail shares common features with outpatient care settings. The problem of hospital-wide scheduling of elective patients addressed in this dissertation can link all health care services provided in Table 3.2.

3.1.2.2   Resources Considered

Table 3.3 provides an aggregate overview whether the selected articles consider single or multiple resources.

Table 3.4 Detailed overview of the resources considered

Ambulatory care services	
Beds	[46]
Clinical services	[18, 46, 174, 203]
Equipment	[44, 45]
Inpatient care services	
Beds	[35, 46, 51]
Services provided by staff	[46, 83]
Transportation resource	[83]
Surgical care services	
Equipment/services	[31, 33, 36, 53, 79, 95, 138, 154]
ICU beds	[95, 140, 154, 216]
OR (general)	[13, 20, 36, 53, 62–65, 79, 95, 136, 138, 140, 147, 163, 181, 186, 216, 227]
OR time/capacity	[31–33, 36, 42, 53–55, 62–65, 79, 95, 113–115, 134, 136, 138, 147, 154, 163, 181, 186, 216, 227]
Other	[165, 186]
Recovery beds	[13, 31–33, 42, 64, 79]
Staff	
Anesthetists	[138]
Nurses	[138]
Surgeons	[20, 33, 36, 42, 62, 64, 65, 79, 95, 136, 147, 181, 186, 216, 227]
Transporters	[13]
Ward capacity	[42, 216]
Residential care services	
Medical devices	[193]
Therapists	[76, 193]
Rooms	[193]

One can observe that the majority of the papers consider multiple resources. For example, Augusto et al. [13] consider operating room capacity as well as recovery beds and transporters. Table 3.4 breaks down the considered resources by each care service and the specific resources therein.

The table reveals that articles predominantly deal with the operating room (OR) as well as its upstream or downstream resources. Another observation is that the majority of the papers that consider inpatient services incorporate beds as a scarce resource. On the contrary, for ambulatory patients, beds are considered less important which is not surprising since ambulatory patients usually leave the hospital at the day when they have their treatment. Moreover, when considering surgical care services, staff such as surgeons are usually considered as scarce resources while, anesthetists or nurses are considered less frequently. This is surprising since, in practice, anesthetists and nurses spend, during surgeries, more time with the patient than surgeons. Another observation is that downstream units such as wards or ICU are considered relatively frequently in the literature but, transporters who guarantee, among other resources, that the patient shows up at the operating room on time are covered rarely in the literature. In contrast to the approaches shown in Table 3.4, the models developed in this dissertation are able to consider all clinical resources such as beds, staff and (operating) rooms as well as equipment.

3.1.2.3   Modelling and Solution Approaches

Since this review focuses on mathematical programming, a detailed overview about the modelling and solution approaches is given in Table 3.5. The table reveals that mixed-integer programming (MIP), in which the models developed in this dissertation can be categorized, is a commonly used modelling and solution method in the field of patient scheduling. Moreover, in order to incorporate uncertainty, stochastic programming is also a commonly used modelling and solution approach.

3.1.2.4   Modelling and Evaluation of Risk

A challenging task in patient scheduling is the incorporation of uncertainty into the planning process. Uncertainty arises for many reasons and examples are uncertain patient arrivals and activity durations. Table 3.6 provides a classification whether or not articles incorporate risk in the planning problem. Moreover, when risk is incorporated, the articles can be divided into the categories whether risk is incorporated into the model (e.g. in terms of scenarios or chance constraints) or whether risk is evaluated in the computational study (e.g. using a simulation). Moreover, each category can be subdivided into which type of risk is considered. The table reveals that most of the articles focus on the deterministic formulation and solution of the problem. However, when risk is considered, activity durations and capacity requirements are the most frequently studied types of uncertainty. In this dissertation, similar to Persson and Persson [163], two types of risk are evaluated in the computational study. Those are uncertain recovery times as well as the capacity requirement by emergency patients.

3.1.2.5   Patient and Resource Related Objectives

Finally, the selected articles can be broken down by patient and resource related objectives. A patient related objective is, for example, that patients should be assigned to a preferred resource such as therapist and ward. A resource related objective is, among others, that utilization has to be maximized. Table 3.7 provides an overview about the patient and resource related objectives and the categorization of the papers. As can be seen, the most popular patient related objective is the minimization of patient waiting time and among the resource related objectives, overtime

Table 3.5 Modelling and solution approach

Mathematical programming	
Branch-and-bound extensions	[31, 147]
Branch-and-cut	[20, 54]
Branch-and-price	[31, 33, 63]
Column-generation	[33, 62–64, 114, 115]
Constraint programming	[138]
Dynamic programming	[33, 115]
Goal programming	[147, 154]
Linear programming	[45, 46, 53, 63, 64, 216]
Mixed-integer programming	[13, 18, 20, 31–33, 35, 36, 42, 44–46, 51, 53, 54, 62–65, 76, 79, 83, 95, 134, 136, 138, 163, 165, 181, 186, 193, 203, 216, 227]
Stochastic programming	[20, 53–55, 113–115, 140, 174]
L-shaped method	[20, 53–55]
Sampling methods	[113–115, 140, 174]
Heuristics	
2-exchange	[181]
First fit decreasing algorithm based	[227]
Hungarian method based	[79]
Lagrangian relaxation based	[13]
Local search	
Tabu search	[35, 76, 113]
Simulated annealing	[35, 76]
Genetic algorithm	[64, 174, 186]
Steepest descent	[76]
Other	[83, 113, 203]
MIP based	[18, 32, 45]
Other	[65]

minimization is the objective that is most frequently considered. Overtime is usually weighted with costs, e.g., for staff. The table also reveals that contribution margin which is maximized in the mathematical models developed in this dissertation has not yet been considered as an objective in the context of patient scheduling.

In what follows, a more detailed examination of a selection of the articles presented in Tables 3.2–3.7 that cover multiple resources and are therefore relevant for this dissertation will be provided. Pham and Klinkert [165] propose a MIP for surgical case scheduling considering scarce resources at the preoperative, perioperative and postoperative stages, solved with the standard solver CPLEX. Augusto et al. [13] consider the problem of scheduling a fixed number of elective cases subject to scarce resources in the operating theater, the post-anesthesia care unit and the patient transportation unit. The problem is modeled as a MIP and solved by using Lagrangian relaxation. Besides the scheduling decision, the model is used to explore the benefit of letting patients recover in the operating room when there is no capacity in the post-anesthesia care unit. Conforti et al. [46] address the so-called

Table 3.6 Modelling of risk

Deterministic	[13, 18, 31–33, 35, 36, 44–46, 51, 62–65, 79, 83, 95, 136, 138, 154, 165, 181, 186, 193, 203, 216, 227]
Risk incorporated into the model	
Activity durations	[20, 53–55, 140, 174]
Capacity requirement	[113–115, 140, 174]
Resource availability	[140]
Risk evaluated in the computational study	
Activity durations	[134, 147, 163]
Arrivals	[163]
Capacity requirement	[42]
Overtime costs	[140]
Priority values	[147]

Table 3.7 Patient and resource related objectives

Patient related	
Minimize	
Penalties	[31–33, 35, 51]
Waiting time of (prioritized) patients	[31–33, 36, 83, 95, 113–115, 140, 147, 174, 181]
Welfare loss	[216]
Maximize	
# patients to be scheduled	[44–46, 193]
Patient satisfaction	[83]
Resource related	
Minimize	
Completion time	[13, 65, 79, 138, 165]
Costs	[18, 20, 53–55, 62–65, 95, 113–115, 140, 174, 186, 203]
Gap between demand & supply	[36]
Maximum workload	[31–33, 42]
Overtime, overutilization	[31–33, 36, 64, 65, 95, 113–115, 138, 140, 147, 154, 174, 181, 186, 203]
Penalties	[35, 51]
Risk of no realization	[134]
Total traveling distance/time	[18, 83, 203]
Underutilization	[83, 174]
Welfare loss	[216]
Maximize	
Preference satisfaction(s)	[154]
Staff collaboration	[138]
Utilization	[64, 65, 136, 147, 154, 163, 227]

"week hospital problem" in which a decision is made if and when elective patients on a waiting list are admitted to the hospital and when the clinical activities of the admitted patients are performed. By definition, the week hospital problem ensures that all admitted patients are discharged in the week they have been admitted. The objective is to maximize the sum of the scores of admitted patients. The planning horizon of 1 week is divided into periods of a half day length. The paper proposes a MIP which is solved with the standard solver CPLEX.

On a tactical planning level, Min and Yih [140] address the surgery scheduling problem for elective patients taking into account stochastic surgery durations and stochastic capacity of the surgical intensive care unit by employing a stochastic discrete program which is solved with the sample average approximation method. Vissers et al. [228] consider the tactical patient mix optimization problem for a single specialty. Employing a MIP, for each day of the week they decide on the number of patients from different categories to be admitted into the hospital. The scarce clinical resources beds (before surgery and for recovery), the operating theater and the intensive care unit are taken into account. The objective is the minimization of the over- and underutilization of the clinical resources. Apart from the recent approaches in operational capacity planning mentioned above, Sepulveda [201] can be regarded as an early work in evaluating DRG-based cost saving policies using simulation.

The models proposed in this dissertation can be categorized into and differentiated from the literature on offline capacity planning of multiple clinical resources as follows. First, an aggregated approach is followed in which clinical activities are assigned to big bucket periods with a length of 1 day. This is similar to Vissers et al. [228] and Conforti et al. [46] and differs from the detailed scheduling approaches of Min and Yih [140] and Pham and Klinkert [165]. However, Vissers et al. [228] decide on the admission date of patients only and assume for the latter a fixed schedule. On the contrary, in this dissertation, patients have to be admitted and their clinical activities are scheduled. Thus, from a hierarchical planning perspective, the developed models are located on a decision level below Vissers et al. [228] but located above the detailed resource planning approaches referenced above. In this respect, the first mathematical program that will be presented in this dissertation uses the decision of Vissers et al. [228] on the patient's admission dates in order to perform a contribution margin-based big bucket scheduling decision, detailing on what day which clinical activities of admitted patients will take place. The second model generalizes the first model by additionally deciding on the day of admission. The decisions made by each of the models can then be employed as input for the detailed resource specific planning approaches in order to decide on more precise schedules and sequences for periods (such as hours or minutes) of less than a day.

Second, with respect to scarce resources (see Tables 3.3 and 3.4), the models developed in this dissertation are, along with Vissers et al. [228], the only ones which consider all scarce clinical resources in an aggregated manner.

Third, in terms of a deterministic or stochastic approach (see Table 3.6), the models developed in this dissertation follow the aggregated approaches of Vissers et al. [228] and Conforti et al. [46]. The problems are modelled as a deterministic MIP using expected values for resource demands of clinical activities, for recovery times and resource capacities. The usage of expected values is well aligned with the big bucket scheduling problem, since deviations of the realized values from the expected values will be mitigated due to variance reduction effects, and there will be no disturbance of detailed time lines. However, with respect to the demand for bed capacity, a deviation from the expected recovery times will disrupt the schedule. Hence, the deterministic models developed in this dissertation are embedded in a rolling horizon approach in order to cope with this type of uncertainty.

Finally, with respect to the objective (see Table 3.7), the developed approaches are the only ones which consider contribution margin, a management accounting measure, and not an operational substitute measure, such as weighted utilization or weighted time which, as we have seen, is already considered exhaustively in the literature.

3.2 The Patient Flow Problem with Fixed Admission Dates

In what follows, the parameters, the decision variables and the model of the patient flow problem with fixed admission dates (PFP-FA) are introduced.

Patients and clinical pathways Let $\mathcal{P}$ denote the set of elective patients that have to be treated in the hospital. It is assumed that for each patient $p \in \mathcal{P}$, the clinical pathway is known which is a standardized, typically evidence based health care process (see van De Klundert et al. [224]). In both models that will be presented, the clinical pathway of a patient is depicted by an activity-on-node graph in which the set of nodes represents the clinical activities and weighted arcs represent minimum time lags between clinical activities.

Let $\mathcal{A}$ denote the set of all clinical activities to be performed and let $\mathcal{E}$ denote the set of all precedence relations between clinical activities. A minimum time lag $(i, j) \in \mathcal{E}$ of weight $d_{i,j}^{\min} \in \mathbb{Z}_{\geq 0}$ stipulates that activity j has to be performed at least $d_{i,j}^{\min}$ periods later than activity i; a period in both models accounts for 1 day. In Sect. 3.4, a detailed example of two patients and their corresponding clinical pathways will be provided. Given the graph $(\mathcal{A}, \mathcal{E})$, the admission period α_p and the discharge activity ϕ_p for each patient $p \in \mathcal{P}$, one can calculate for each activity $i \in \mathcal{A}$ the earliest period E_i and the latest period L_i in which the activity has to be performed with longest path methods (see, for example, Neumann et al. [145]; details of the calculation are given in Sect. 4.2.1). Let $\mathcal{W}_i := \{E_i, E_i + 1, \ldots, L_i\}$ denote the time window of activity i and let $\mathcal{T}$ be the set of periods (days) within the planning horizon. The length of the planning horizon $|\mathcal{T}|$ is set to the maximum latest period of all activities $\max_{i \in \mathcal{A}} L_i$ which equals the latest discharge period of all patients.

Hospital resources Scarce hospital resources are depicted by two sets, day resources and overnight resources. The set of day resources $\mathcal{R}^d$ depicts all resources which are available during regular working days, such as computer tomography scanner (CT), magnetic resonance imaging scanner (MRI), operating room (OR) and intensive care unit (ICU). Each day resource $k \in \mathcal{R}^d$ has a capacity $R_{k,t}$ in period $t \in \mathcal{T}$. The capacity demand of activity $i \in \mathcal{A}$ on day resource $k \in \mathcal{R}^d$ is $r_{i,k}$. $R_{k,t}$ and $r_{i,k}$ are typically measured in minutes. The capacity demand $r_{i,k}$ of clinical activities ranges between several minutes and several hours, whereas the capacity of day resources is, in the case of a single shift, 8 h. The set of overnight resources is depicted by $\mathcal{R}^n$. Overnight resources represent beds available at specialties, for example, the number of beds available at the surgical specialty.

The number of beds available at overnight resource $k \in \mathcal{R}^n$ in period $t \in \mathcal{T}$ is $R_{k,t}$. If patient $p \in \mathcal{P}$ stays in the hospital from day t to day $t + 1$, he requires one bed from the overnight resource b_p in period t. $\mathcal{R} := \mathcal{R}^d \cup \mathcal{R}^n$ denotes the set of all resources, day and overnight resources.

DRG and contribution margin In this dissertation, a DRG system is considered in which, given a patient's DRG and his admission day, the hospital receives a specific revenue which depends on the DRG and the discharge date and thus the length of stay. Figure 3.1a, b show two length of stay and DRG dependent revenue functions for a specific DRG (based on the German DRG system).

The revenue (dotted line) is constant if the length of stay (LOS) is between a low LOS trim point and a high LOS trim point. The trim points, 2 and 9 in Fig. 3.1a, b, represent the length of stay range for the majority of the patients with a "normal" healing process. In the case of a length of stay below the low LOS trim point there is a per-day reduction of the revenue. In this scenario, the health insurance company takes into account the fact that the hospital has lower costs than for the average patient with the same DRG. In contrast, if for medical reasons the length of stay of a patient is above the high LOS trim point, the hospital receives a per-day surcharge on top of the fixed revenue in order to compensate additional costs (see case (a) in Fig. 3.1 for an LOS of 10 or 11 days). Further, if the patient's length of stay is already above the high LOS trim point and further LOSs are not medically justified, this surcharge will not be paid. In Fig. 3.1a this holds true for LOSs greater than 11 days. Correspondingly, if the patient is an "inlier" which means that his LOS is between the low and high LOS trim point (see Schreyögg et al. [194]) then the surcharge will not be paid, either (see case (b) in Fig. 3.1). In practice, a claims agent of the health insurance company scrutinizes the bill, examines the medical record and then makes a decision regarding the surcharge.

Table 3.8 provides an overview of the DRG-based reimbursement policies of different countries.

The table reveals that high LOS trim points exist in all listed countries while low LOS trim points are only in place in some of the countries. A reason for countries not to employ low LOS trim points is to provide an incentive to admit short-stay visits or day-cases (for example in England, see Schreyögg et al. [194]). The parameter of the revenue function, low and high LOS trim points, fixed revenue as well as per day reduction and addition are DRG specific (see for example Porter and Guth [172]). Since the length of stay is measured in discrete days, the revenue function is discrete

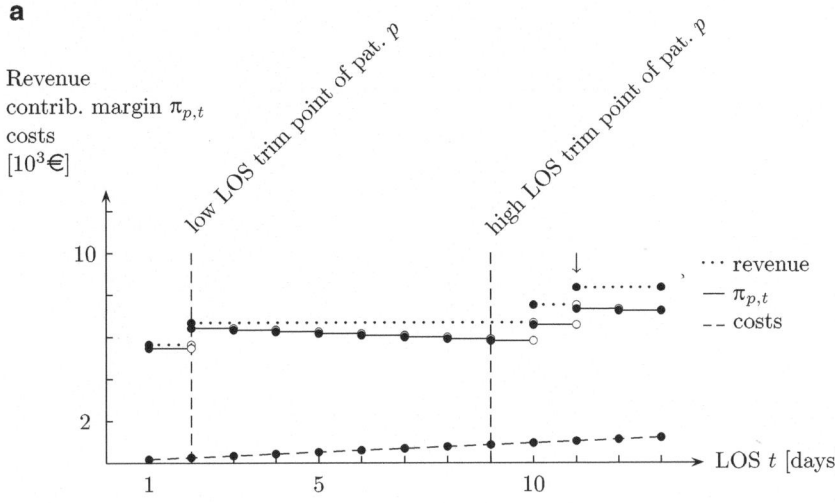

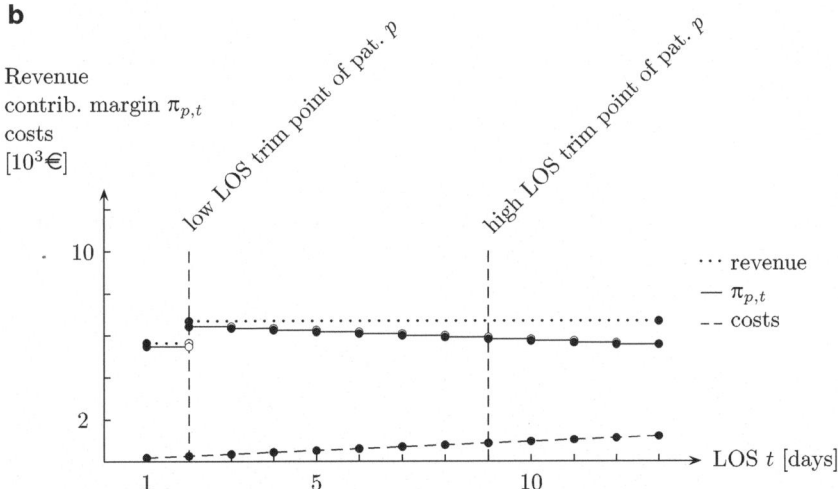

Fig. 3.1 Two example revenue, cost and contribution (contrib.) margin functions. **(a)** Revenue including per day surcharge for reaching the first and the second day after the high LOS trim point. **(b)** Constant revenue after reaching the low LOS trim point

as well. From the revenue, the variable costs not associated with clinical procedures are subtracted. Therefore, the focus is only on costs such as washing and cleaning (dashed line in Fig. 3.1a, b). By this, the contribution margin $\pi_{p,t-\alpha_p}$ for patient p with admission day α_p, discharge day t and thus length of stay $t - \alpha_p$ (solid line in Fig. 3.1a, b) is obtained. Note that the costs for clinical procedures are not subtracted because, in accordance with the clinical pathway, the latter will be undertaken in any case and are therefore not relevant for the decision, whereas the patients' length of stay is a function of the scheduling decision. Also note that the time-constant

Table 3.8 DRG-based reimbursement policies of different countries

Country	Low LOS trim point	High LOS trim point	Reference
Australia	Yes	Yes	Sharma [204]
Austria	Yes	Yes	Busse et al. [29]
Canada	No	Yes	Botz [23]
Denmark	No	Yes	Schreyögg et al. [194]
England	No	Yes	Schreyögg et al. [194]
France	Yes	Yes	Schreyögg et al. [194]
Germany	Yes	Yes	Schreyögg et al. [194]
Italy	No	Yes	Schreyögg et al. [194]
Spain	No	Yes	Schreyögg et al. [194]
Switzerland	Yes	Yes (2)	Zaugg et al. [242]
USA	No	Yes	Rogers et al. [185]

DRG variant, which is relevant for DRG systems where no trim points exist, is a special case of the time-variable variant and, hence, the models developed in this dissertation can be applied directly to the latter.

Decision variables and model formulation Using the binary variables

$$x_{i,t} = \begin{cases} 1, & \text{if clinical activity } i \in \mathcal{A} \text{ is done at day } t \in \mathcal{W}_i \\ 0, & \text{otherwise} \end{cases}$$

originally introduced by Pritsker et al. [173], the patient flow problem with fixed admission date (PFP-FA) can be modelled as follows:

$$\text{Maximize} \quad z = \sum_{p \in \mathcal{P}} \sum_{t \in \mathcal{W}_{\phi_p}} \pi_{p,t-\alpha_p} \cdot x_{\phi_p,t} \tag{3.1}$$

subject to

$$\sum_{t \in \mathcal{W}_j} t \cdot x_{j,t} \geq \sum_{t \in \mathcal{W}_i} t \cdot x_{i,t} + d_{i,j}^{\min} \qquad \forall (i,j) \in \mathcal{E} \tag{3.2}$$

$$\sum_{i \in \mathcal{A}: t \in \mathcal{W}_i} r_{i,k} \cdot x_{i,t} \leq R_{k,t} \qquad \forall k \in \mathcal{R}^d, t \in \mathcal{T} \tag{3.3}$$

$$\sum_{p \in \mathcal{P}: b_p = k, t \geq \alpha_p} \left(1 - \sum_{\tau = E_{\phi_p}}^{\min\{t, L_{\phi_p}\}} x_{\phi_p,\tau} \right) \leq R_{k,t} \qquad \forall k \in \mathcal{R}^n, t \in \mathcal{T} \tag{3.4}$$

$$\sum_{t \in \mathcal{W}_i} x_{i,t} = 1 \qquad \forall i \in \mathcal{A} \tag{3.5}$$

$$x_{i,t} \in \{0, 1\} \qquad \forall i \in \mathcal{A}, t \in \mathcal{W}_i \tag{3.6}$$

Table 3.9 Bed allocation for the PFP-FA

t		1	2	3	4	5	6	7
$x_{\phi_1,t}$		–	–	–	–	0	1	0
$\sum\limits_{b_1=1,t\geq1}\left(1-\sum\limits_{\tau=E_{\phi_1}}^{\min\{t,L_{\phi_1}\}}x_{\phi_1,\tau}\right)$		1	1	1	1	1	0	0

The objective function (3.1) maximizes the contribution margin of all patients who have to be admitted to the hospital. Constraints (3.2) ensure minimum time lags between clinical activities. Note that for $d_{i,j}^{\min} = 0$ activities i and j can be performed on the same day. This might be e.g. the case for two diagnostic activities. Constraints (3.3) depict the limited capacity of day resources. For each resource and day, the capacity demand of all activities performed at that day must not exceed resource capacity. Note that the dimension of resource capacity can be, for example, time or slots in a master surgical schedule. Constraints (3.4) denote the resource constraints for overnight resources. For patient p, the bed allocation starts with the fixed admission date α_p and the discharge activity ϕ_p releases the bed. Constraints (3.5) ensure that each activity is assigned to exactly one period of its time window. Variable definitions are provided in (3.6).

Table 3.9 provides an example of the bed allocation with a planning horizon of $\mathcal{T} := \{1, \ldots, 7\}$ days, overnight resource $\mathcal{R}^n := \{1\}$ and a single patient $\mathcal{P} := \{1\}$ with admission date $\alpha_1 = 1$ requiring overnight resource $b_1 = 1$. The first row provides the decision variables $x_{\phi_1,t}$ for discharge activity ϕ_1 of patient 1 which has to take place in exactly one period within the time window $\mathcal{W}_{\phi_1} := \{5, 6, 7\}$. As can be seen, the PFP-FA selects the discharge period 6 by setting $x_{\phi_1,6} = 1$. The second row gives the left hand side of constraints (3.4) for patient 1. The patient requires a bed starting with the night between days 1 and 2 until the night between days 5 and 6.

In contrast to resource-constrained project scheduling (see Pritsker et al. [173]), the PFP-FA does not undertake detailed scheduling in which an activity's starting and ending time is precisely planned. Instead, the PFP-FA does aggregated planning by assigning activities to days instead of deciding on activity start and finish times during the day. This aggregated view can be illustrated by the relation between the length of periods and the duration of activities. In resource-constrained project scheduling, we typically have activity durations which are multiples of a period. Conversely, in the case of the models developed in this dissertation, activity durations are between 10 min and several hours, whereas the length of one period is a working day with, in the case of one shift, 8 h. The approach of this mathematical program can thus be compared to assembly line balancing (see for example Boysen et al. [26]) in which tasks are assigned to stations but no sequencing of tasks within stations is undertaken.

Note that model (3.1)–(3.6) does not take into account a master surgery schedule (MSS) in which OR capacity is assigned on the basis of a day or half-days to specialties but assumes that surgeries from any specialty can be undertaken any day.

However, the model can be generalized straightforwardly in order to take MSSs into account. For this, constraints (3.3) have to be defined not for the aggregated single day resource "operating theatre" but for each specialty. In consequence, the number of constraints (3.3) increases.

The number of binary decision variables is $\sum_{i \in \mathcal{A}} |\mathcal{W}_i|$ while the number of constraints is $|\mathcal{E}| + |\mathcal{R}| \cdot |\mathcal{T}| + |\mathcal{A}|$. For a realistic problem with a planning horizon of $|\mathcal{T}| = 28$ days, $|\mathcal{P}| = 150$ patients, $|\mathcal{R}| = 10$ resources, 3 activities per patient, time window size of $|\mathcal{W}_i| = 3$ days for each activity $i \in \mathcal{A}$ and $|\mathcal{E}| = 300$ precedence relations, we have 1,350 binary decision variables and 1,030 constraints. Tables 4.38–4.40 provide the problem sizes of real-world test instances.

3.3   The Patient Flow Problem with Variable Admission Dates

In the case of elective patients, the admission date is typically negotiated between the patient or the referring physician and the hospital. Hence, α_p is no longer a parameter. Instead, for each patient p, an admission activity σ_p is introduced which has to be assigned by variables $x_{\sigma_p,t}$ to exactly one admission day t within time window $\mathcal{W}_{\sigma_p}$. Note that in the case of variable admission dates, the contribution margin function $\pi_{p,t}$ for patient $p \in \mathcal{P}$ is defined for lengths of stay $t \in \mathcal{L}_p$, calculated by subtracting the admission date from the discharge date, formally given by

$$\sum_{t \in \mathcal{W}_{\phi_p}} t \cdot x_{\phi_p,t} - \sum_{t \in \mathcal{W}_{\sigma_p}} t \cdot x_{\sigma_p,t}. \tag{3.7}$$

In order to ease the readability of the model, binary variables

$$y_{p,t} = \begin{cases} 1, & \text{if patient } p \in \mathcal{P} \text{ has a LOS of } t \in \mathcal{L}_p \text{ days} \\ 0, & \text{otherwise.} \end{cases}$$

are introduced where $\mathcal{L}_p$ denotes the set of possible LOSs of patient p.

Now, the patient flow problem with variable admission dates (PFP-VA) can be formulated as follows:

$$\text{Maximize} \quad z = \sum_{p \in \mathcal{P}} \sum_{t \in \mathcal{L}_p} \pi_{p,t} \cdot y_{p,t} \tag{3.8}$$

subject to (3.2)–(3.3), (3.5)–(3.6) and

Table 3.10 Bed allocation for the PFP-VA

$t \in \mathcal{T}$	1	2	3	4	5	6	7
$x_{\sigma_1,t}$	1	0	0	–	–	–	–
$x_{\phi_1,t}$	–	–	–	–	1	0	0
$\displaystyle\sum_{b_1=1}\left(\sum_{\tau=E_{\sigma_1}}^{\min\{t,L_{\sigma_1}\}} x_{\sigma_1,\tau} - \sum_{\tau=E_{\phi_1}}^{\min\{t,L_{\phi_1}\}} x_{\phi_1,\tau}\right)$	1	1	1	1	0	0	0

$$\sum_{p\in\mathcal{P}:b_p=k}\left(\sum_{\tau=E_{\sigma p}}^{\min\{t,L_{\sigma p}\}} x_{\sigma p,\tau} - \sum_{\tau=E_{\phi p}}^{\min\{t,L_{\phi p}\}} x_{\phi p,\tau}\right) \le R_{k,t} \quad \forall k\in\mathcal{R}^n, t\in\mathcal{T} \tag{3.9}$$

$$\sum_{t\in\mathcal{W}_{\phi p}} t\cdot x_{\phi p,t} - \sum_{t\in\mathcal{W}_{\sigma p}} t\cdot x_{\sigma p,t} = \sum_{t\in\mathcal{L}_p} t\cdot y_{p,t} \quad\quad \forall p\in\mathcal{P} \tag{3.10}$$

$$\sum_{t\in\mathcal{L}_p} y_{p,t} = 1 \quad\quad \forall p\in\mathcal{P} \tag{3.11}$$

$$y_{p,t} \in \{0,1\} \quad\quad \forall p\in\mathcal{P}, t\in\mathcal{L}_p \tag{3.12}$$

Objective function (3.8) maximizes the contribution margin of all patients. Overnight resource constraints (3.9) have been modified in order to take into account variable admission dates. Constraints (3.10) denote that LOS is the difference between the start of the discharge activity and the start of the admission activity. Constraints (3.11) ensure that for each patient exactly one LOS is selected and decision variables for each patient and LOS are defined by (3.12).

Table 3.10 provides an extension of the example in Table 3.9 where, additionally, for patient 1 the admission time window $\mathcal{W}_{\sigma_1} := \{1,2,3\}$ is assumed. The first row provides the decision variables for the admission activity σ_1 of patient 1 as well as the decision of PFP-VA to admit patient 1 in the first period ($x_{\sigma_1,1} = 1$). The second row gives the time window for the discharge activity as well as the decision of PFP-VA to discharge patient 1 in period 5 ($x_{\phi_1,5} = 1$). The third row provides the left hand side of the bed allocation constraints (3.9).

The number of binary decision variables of model PFP-VA is $\sum_{i\in\mathcal{A}} |\mathcal{W}_i| + \sum_{p\in\mathcal{P}} |\mathcal{L}_p|$ and the number of constraints is $|\mathcal{E}| + |\mathcal{R}| \cdot |\mathcal{T}| + 2\cdot|\mathcal{P}| + |\mathcal{A}|$. Thus, PFP-VA is considerably larger than PFP-FA. For example, consider the problem instance in Sect. 3.2 with an additional admission activity per patient and $|\mathcal{L}_p| = 3$ possible LOSs for each patient $p \in \mathcal{P}$. Then, the number of precedence relations is $|\mathcal{E}| = 450$, the number of binary decision variables is 1,800 and the number of constraints is 1,630. For real-world instances, again, see Tables 4.38–4.40.

Table 3.11 Activities (a) and resources (b)

a

$i \in \mathcal{A}$		Description
PFP-FA	PFP-VA	
–	1	Admission of pat. 1
2	2	Spine CT for pat. 1
3	3	Spinal surgery of pat. 1
4	4	Discharge of pat. 1
–	5	Admission of pat. 2
6	6	Arteriography for pat. 2
7	7	Stent implantation of pat. 2
8	8	Discharge of pat. 2

b

$k \in \mathcal{R}$	Description	$R_{k,t}$
1	Radiology unit	30 min. on workdays, 0 otherwise
2	Operating theater	100 min. on workdays, 0 otherwise
3	Surgical ward	2 beds on workdays, 1 otherwise

3.4 An Example of the Patient Flow Problem with Fixed and Variable Admission Dates

In what follows, an example with two patients will be provided. Patient (pat.) $p = 1$ has the DRG I53Z (spinal disc surgery) and patient 2 has the DRG B04D (extracranial surgery). Consider $\mathcal{T} := \{1, \ldots, 7\}$ time periods, activities $i \in \mathcal{A}$ and resources $\mathcal{R}^d := \{1, 2\}$ and $\mathcal{R}^n := \{3\}$ as shown in Table 3.11. The overnight resource requirements are $b_1 = b_2 = 3$. Clinical pathways and resource requirements for day resources are shown in Fig. 3.2.

In Fig. 3.2a, b, $r_{7,2} = 100$ denotes that activity 7 (stent implantation for patient 2) requires 100 min from day resource 2 which is the operating theater. The minimum time lag $d_{3,4}^{\min} = 4$ between activity 3 and 4 in Fig. 3.2a, b denotes that at least 4 days of recovery time have to pass between the surgery and the discharge of patient 1. For the PFP-FA let the admission days for both patients be $\alpha_1 = \alpha_2 = 1$. Table 3.12 provides earliest and latest time periods to schedule the activities as obtained by longest path calculation.

Table 3.13 shows the contribution margins for the two patients. Note that with increasing t, this margin decreases.

Solving the PFP-FA and the PFP-VA with the given parameters, the optimal solutions presented in Fig. 3.3a, b are obtained.

The optimal objective function value of the PFP-FA and the PFP-VA is € 7,210.21 and € 7,271.08, respectively. Note that in the case of fixed admission dates, the length of stay of patient 1 is 1 day longer than in the case of variable

Fig. 3.2 Clinical pathways
for the PFP-FA (**a**) and the
PFP-VA (**b**)

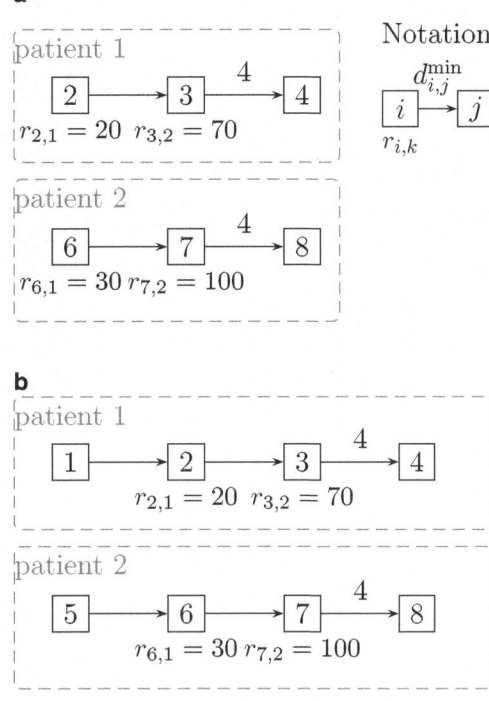

Table 3.12 Earliest and latest periods for the PFP-FA (a) and the PFP-VA (b)

a							**b**								
$i \in \mathcal{A}$	2	3	4	6	7	8	$i \in \mathcal{A}$	1	2	3	4	5	6	7	8
E_i	1	1	5	1	1	5	E_i	1	1	1	5	1	1	1	5
L_i	3	3	7	3	3	7	L_i	3	3	3	7	3	3	3	7

Table 3.13 Contribution
margin (in €) for the PFP-FA
and the PFP-VA

t	4	5	6
$\pi_{1,t}$	3,772.67	3,711.80	3,650.94
$\pi_{2,t}$	3,498.41	3,436.15	3,373.90

Fig. 3.3 Optimal solution for
the PFP-FA (**a**) and the
PFP-VA (**b**)

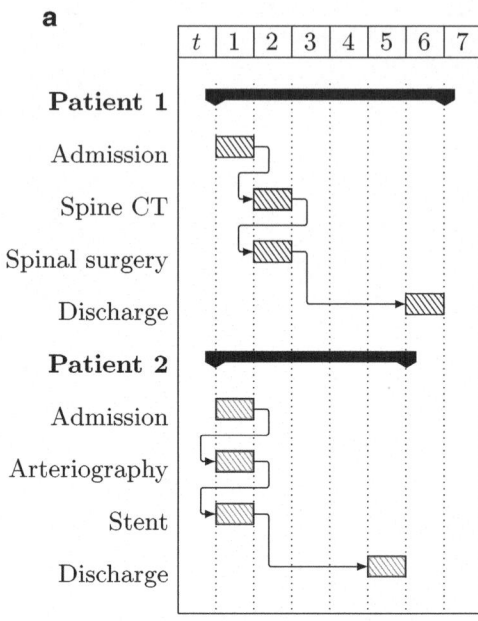

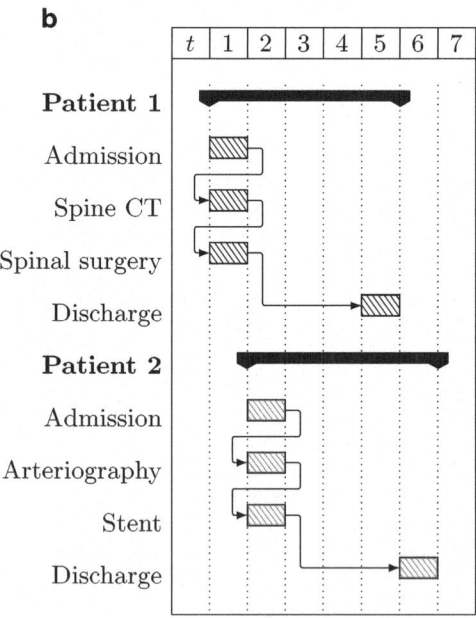

admission dates. The admission date and the discharge date of patient 2 are postponed by 1 day in the case of flexible admission dates, resulting in the same length of stay as in the fixed case.

3.5   A Rolling Horizon Approach for Scheduling the Hospital-Wide Flow of Elective Patients

In practice, there is considerable variance in the data and therefore hospitals cannot undertake a flow management of patients for a whole month in advance. Instead, they have to embed the model into a rolling horizon approach in which the planning of the patient flow is done every day with the most recent information available. This is already done in practice. Here, the hospital undertakes daily allocation decisions for single resources, such as the operating theater and the wards. For example, each afternoon a decision is made about which of the patients will be considered for surgery on the next day. Therefore, each of the two patient flow models are embedded in a rolling horizon approach in which each problem instance is solved each day. In each run, the most recent data is used. This is deterministic data which is available at the day of planning, such as planned admissions in the PFP-FA, or stochastic data for which expected values are calculated. A detailed description of the rolling horizon procedure of the PFP-FA will be given which can directly be adapted to the PFP-VA.

Each iteration of the rolling horizon planning is denoted by θ, initialized to $\theta := 0$ at the beginning, and incremented after each iteration by $\theta \leftarrow \theta + 1$. Let S_i^θ be the vector of start times for activities $i \in \mathcal{A}$ obtained by solving the instances for each rolling horizon iteration θ. Let δ be a look-ahead parameter where information about arriving elective patients can be assumed to be complete. The activity that induces recovery for patient $p \in \mathcal{P}$ is denoted by ρ_p. The set $\mathcal{A}_p \subset \mathcal{A}$ denotes an ordered tuple $(1, \ldots, \rho_p, \ldots, \phi_p)$ of activities that belong to patient $p \in \mathcal{P}$. $E[\varrho_p]$ is the expected recovery time which is continuously updated employing a naive Bayes approach as described in Sect. 2.3.1. The $\hat{\varrho}_p$ is the DRG dependent observed maximum recovery time of patient $p \in \mathcal{P}$. The expected capacity of resource $k \in \mathcal{R}$ on day $t \in \mathcal{T}$ is denoted by $E[R_{k,t}]$. The realization of remaining capacity available for elective patients is denoted by $R_{k,t}^{\text{real}}$. More precisely, it is assumed that complete information about the realized capacity is available only for the beginning of the rolling horizon (day $t = 1$). Thus, $R_{k,1}^{\text{real}}$ is considered instead of $E[R_{k,1}]$. Next, we have the surgery lead time ϖ_p which is 1, if patient $p \in \mathcal{P}$ has to wait at least 1 day from the admission until the surgery date. Otherwise, $\varpi_p = 0$. The rolling horizon procedure is shown in Fig. 3.4.

Initially, the expected resource capacity $E[R_{k,t}]$ is determined by a quantile of the week-day dependent remaining resource capacity for elective patients in the hospital data. Next, patients which arrive in interval $[1; \theta + \delta]$ are generated. Their activities and further parameters such as precedence relations are adapted. At the

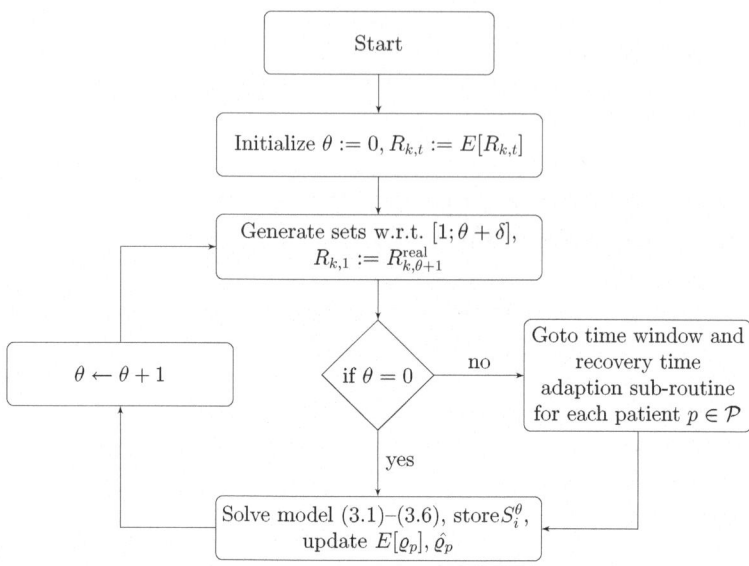

Fig. 3.4 Rolling horizon procedure

same step, the remaining resource capacity is set for the first day of the rolling horizon planning $t = 1$. Afterwards, time windows (amongst remaining recovery times), precedence relations and time lags are recalculated. Then, the instance is solved and the schedule is stored for each day θ in vectors S_i^θ.

Figure 3.5 shows the procedure for adapting time windows during each iteration θ of the rolling horizon planning. The first decision node is used to check, whether or not patients have been discharged in earlier iterations of the rolling horizon planning procedure. If the discharge activity ϕ_p of patient $p \in \mathcal{P}$ has been scheduled for the first day for any period $1 \leq \tau \leq \theta$, all time windows for all activities $i \in \mathcal{A}_p$ are empty which is ensured by Eqs. (3.13). Therefore, those activities can no longer be scheduled. The next decision node is used to check for period θ, whether the patient has been admitted, is planned for admission, or will be admitted in future periods. Patient $p \in \mathcal{P}$ will be admitted in the future if $\theta < \alpha_p$. For future admissions, we follow the left arc of the decision node and adapt the admission date α_p of patient $p \in \mathcal{P}$ according to the current iteration θ by using Eq. (3.23). Based on this, the respective time windows and recovery times are set according to Eqs. (3.24)–(3.28). If patient $p \in \mathcal{P}$ is admitted in the current period or has been admitted, the final decision node is reached. Here it is checked, whether recovery induction activity ρ_p has been scheduled. If a surgery has not yet been undertaken, the earliest start dates of all activities of the pre-recovery stage of patient $p \in \mathcal{P}$ are set to 1 by using Eqs. (3.17). Activities $\rho_p \leq i < \phi_p$ cannot start before $1 + \varpi_p$ because of a potential surgery preparation time after the admission of patient $p \in \mathcal{P}$. Accordingly, the earliest start dates are set by using Eqs. (3.18) and (3.19) while the earliest discharge date is set by Eq. (3.20). The latest discharge

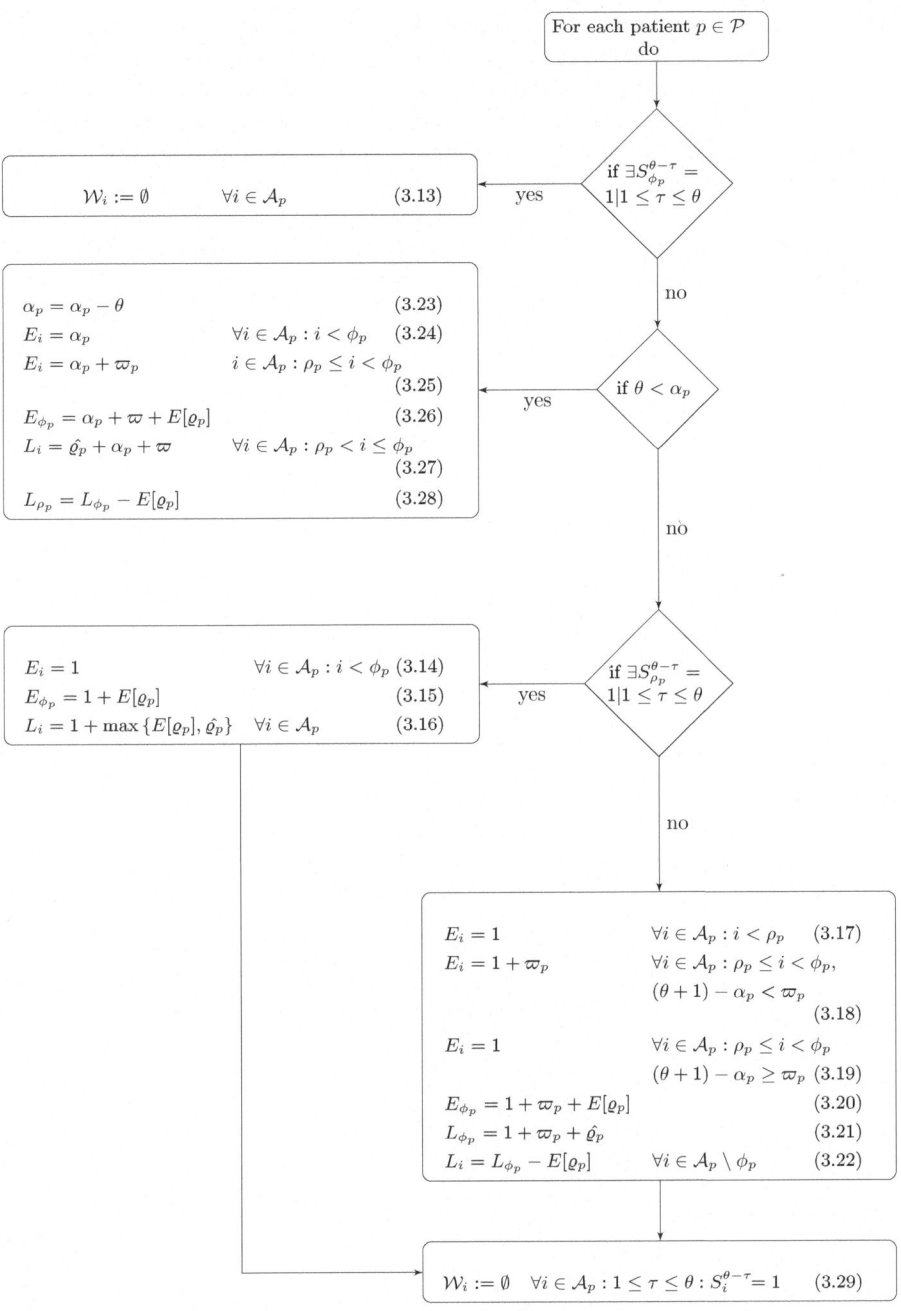

Fig. 3.5 Time window adaption sub-routine

date is set by Eq. (3.21). The latest start of all other activities is set by Eqs. (3.22). Next, we turn to the case when the patient is in the recovery stage (left-hand side of the third decision node). Using Eqs. (3.14), the earliest start dates of all activities except the discharge activity are set to period 1. The earliest discharge date is set by Eq. (3.15). Note that the recovery stage may be over but not all activities (e.g. post surgical activities) have been scheduled for patient $p \in \mathcal{P}$ yet. Therefore, the latest start of all other activities is set by Eqs. (3.16). Finally, Eqs. (3.29) ensure that the time windows of all activities that have been scheduled in former periods of the rolling horizon are empty.

Chapter 4
Experimental Analyses

The structure of this chapter is as follows: In the first section, a thorough analysis of the presented machine learning methods for early DRG classification and its comparison with a DRG grouper is provided. In the second section, a computational and economic analysis of scheduling the hospital-wide patient flow of elective patients is given.

4.1 Experimental Evaluation of the Early DRG Classification

For the experimental investigation of the early DRG classification, different assumptions are made in order to generate datasets that will be used to analyze the performance of the DRG grouper and the machine learning methods. Results of the attribute ranking and selection techniques as well as the classification performance are shown. The results are broken down by MDCs and by DRGs. Finally, an evaluation of misclassification costs is provided.

4.1.1 Data from Patients That Contact the Hospital Before Admission (Elective Patients)

The data gathered from the collaborating county hospital Erding contains information about 3,458 elective patients that contacted the hospital before admission and were assigned to 413 different DRGs. The frequency distribution of the 50 most

Reprinted by permission, Daniel Gartner, Rainer Kolisch, Daniel B. Neill and Rema Padman, Machine Learning Approaches for Early DRG Classification and Resource Allocation, INFORMS Journal on Computing. Copyright 2015, the Institute for Operations Research and the Management Sciences, 5521 Research Park Drive, Suite 200, Catonsville, Maryland 21228 USA.

D. Gartner, *Optimizing Hospital-wide Patient Scheduling*, Lecture Notes in Economics and Mathematical Systems 674, DOI 10.1007/978-3-319-04066-0_4,
© Springer International Publishing Switzerland 2014

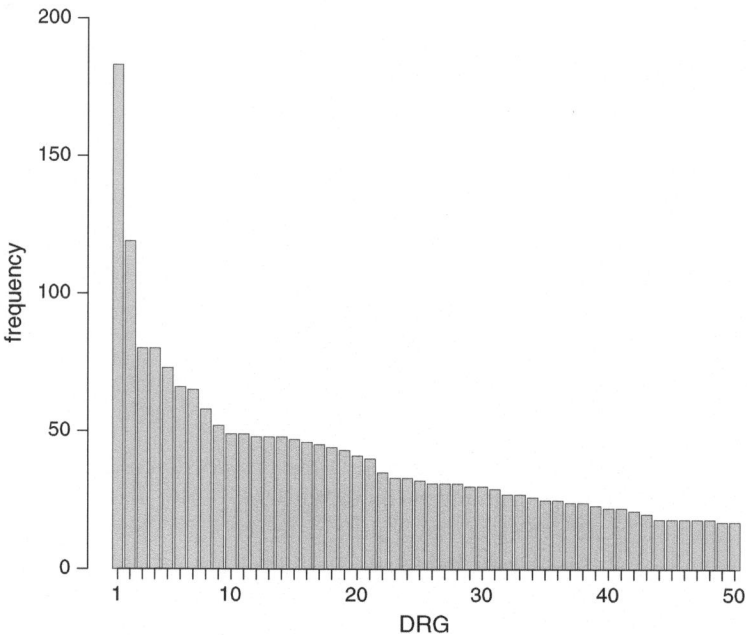

Fig. 4.1 DRG frequency distribution for elective patients

Table 4.1 Information documented before admission

# attributes	Description
79	Appointment-specific and demographic information (e.g. age, referring physician, admission priority)
149	Clinical information (free-text)
4	DRG information predicted by the DRG grouper (DRG, 2 DRG substrings, complication and co-morbidity level (CCL))

frequent DRGs for this group of patients is provided in Fig. 4.1. DRG codes were replaced by natural numbers $(1, \ldots, 50)$. The figure reveals a quick DRG frequency dropoff. Moreover, the 35 most frequent DRGs account for more than 50.4 % of all elective inpatients. Within this group of patients, the three most frequent DRGs are: "Non-surgical therapy of the spine column, age >65 years" $(n = 183)$, "Non-surgical therapy of the spine column, age ≤65 years" $(n = 119)$ and "Medium complex cardiovascular incision" $(n = 80)$. Table 4.1 provides a summary of the attributes used in the study for the DRG classification before admission. For a detailed description of the attributes, see Table B.1.

The procedure for extracting attributes from free-text is as follows: Initially, all strings are converted to lower case. Afterwards, a word tokenizer and stopwords are employed to filter out irrelevant characters and words, respectively. Then, a lower threshold for the term frequency is set in order to obtain a sufficiently large representation of relevant strings. Finally, in the case of free-text diagnoses, word

Table 4.2 Datasets generated for the DRG classification before admission

Procedure codes	Admission diagnoses	Dataset
All codes	All	1
	"Admission diagnosis 1" only	2
	None	3
All codes documented within the first 2 days	All	4
	"Admission diagnosis 1" only	5
	None	6
All codes documented in the first day	All	7
	"Admission diagnosis 1" only	8
	None	9
None	All	10
	"Admission diagnosis 1" only	11
	None	12

stemming is employed. Although the patients' gender is not documented before admission, the assumption is made that this attribute is available for the DRG grouper and for the machine learning methods because the name of the patient usually informs the admitting nurse of the patient's gender and, if unclear, the gender could be reported over the telephone.

In what follows, a description of generating scenarios when more information could be available before admission, in particular diagnoses and clinical procedures, is provided. Datasets are generated that represent scenarios about the availability of further information as presented in Table 4.2. For example, employing dataset 2, the hypothesis is that, in addition to the attributes available at first contact (see Table B.1), all procedure codes of the episode documented after admission and the "admission diagnosis 1" are available for each patient in the dataset. Accordingly, the corresponding medical partition and category code of "admission diagnosis 1" are available as well since they can be derived directly from the ICD code. None of these scenarios are unrealistic since, if a referring physician contacts the hospital, e.g., because of a necessary hernia repair for his patient, structured information about the patient could directly be transmitted to the hospital where the whole evidence-based care process and the scheduling of all necessary activities for hernia repair will be started.

4.1.2 Data from All Patients Available at Admission (Elective and Non-elective Patients)

When focusing on both, elective and non-elective patients at admission, the dataset gathered from the collaborating hospital is considerably larger. More precisely, 16,601 elective and non-elective patients were admitted during the year 2011 and were assigned to 680 different DRGs which is more than 1.6 times the number of

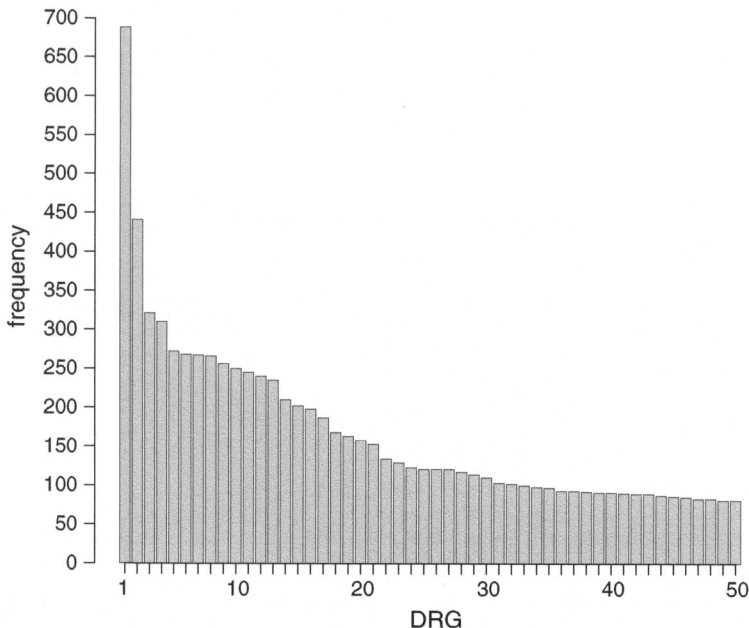

Fig. 4.2 DRG frequency distribution for all patients

DRGs within the elective patient data before admission. The frequency distribution of the 50 most frequent DRGs of all (elective and non-elective) patients ordered by decreasing frequency is provided in Fig. 4.2. DRG codes were replaced by natural numbers $(1, \ldots, 50)$, too.

In contrast to the group of elective patients, the three most frequent DRGs are: "Esophagitis" $(n = 688)$, which is a disorder of the esophagus, "childbirth" $(n = 441)$ and "collapse or heart disease" $(n = 321)$. Similar to the observation for elective patients, the figure reveals a quick DRG frequency dropoff. Moreover, the 50 most frequent DRGs account for more than 50.1 % of all inpatients. In order to evaluate the accuracy of the assignment of the primary diagnosis to the patient at admission, Fig. 4.3 presents for each patient a matching of the primary diagnosis assigned by the hospital at admission vs. the primary diagnosis assigned by the hospital at discharge for the purpose of accounting-driven DRG classification (see Sect. 1.1). The axes of the figure reveal that the number of different primary diagnoses assigned at admission is less than the number of primary diagnoses assigned at discharge, which implies that the precision of the different diagnosis codes is higher at discharge than at admission. A second observation is that the primary diagnosis assigned to each patient at admission very frequently matches the primary diagnosis assigned to each patient at discharge (in approximately 55.6 % of the cases). At its mid-right part, the figure reveals a relatively broad vertical bar which represents particulary patients who were assigned a diagnosis of the ICD category "symptoms and abnormal clinical and laboratory findings, not specified"

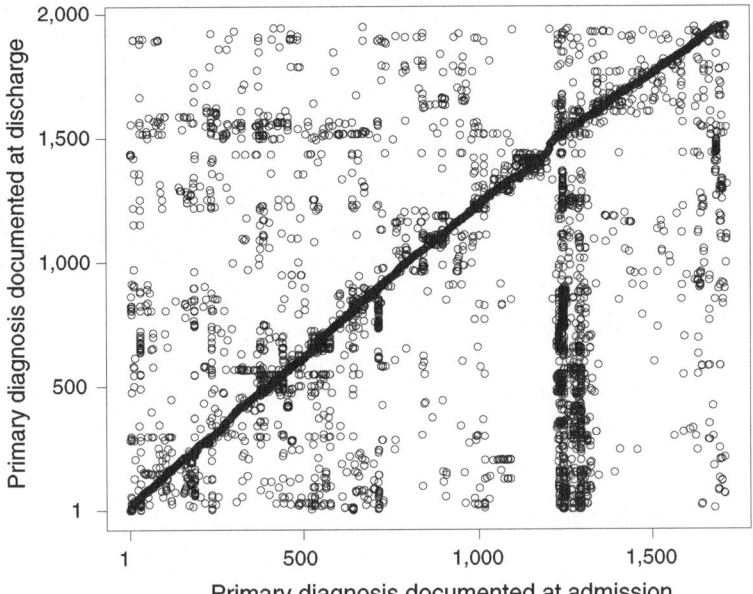

Fig. 4.3 Assignment of admission vs. discharge diagnoses to all patients

Table 4.3 Information documented at admission

# attributes	Description
10	Demographic information (e.g. type of and reason for admission, age in days in case of newborns)
18	Diagnostic information (6 admission diagnoses coded by ICD and the corresponding medical partition and category code)
4	DRG information predicted by the DRG grouper (DRG, 2 DRG substrings, CCL)

at admission. In practice, when this kind of patient shows up at the hospital, many diagnostic steps have to be undertaken until the actual primary diagnosis, which is necessary for DRG-grouping, can be determined and assigned to the patient. In conclusion, a DRG grouper can be considered ill-suited for early DRG classification for at least 44.4 % of the patients and in particular for patients admitted with unspecific laboratory findings.

Table 4.3 provides a summary of the attributes used in the study for the DRG classification at admission. For a detailed description of the attributes, see Table B.1.

Similar to the DRG classification before admission, four datasets which represent scenarios of data that could be made available at admission are generated. An overview is presented in Table 4.4.

Naturally, since admission diagnoses are available at admission time, datasets 13–16 represent variations of clinical procedures only, instead of additionally varying information about diagnoses. For example, employing dataset 15, the

Table 4.4 Datasets
generated for the DRG
classification at admission

Procedure codes	Dataset
All codes	13
All codes documented within the first 2 days	14
All codes documented in the first day	15
None	16

hypothesis is that, in addition to the attributes presented in Table 4.3 and B.1, all procedure codes that are documented in the first day would be available for each patient in the dataset. Similar to the datasets generated before admission, none of these scenarios are unrealistic because when an emergency patient is to be treated at the hospital, the preparation of some procedures (e.g. surgeries) is already performed prior to the patient's arrival, for example, when emergency physicians contact the hospital from the ambulance vehicle.

4.1.3 Results of the Attribute Ranking and Selection

In what follows, the results of the attribute ranking and selection before and at admission are provided. As suggested by Robnik-Šikonja and Kononenko [184], the parameter k for the nearest hits or misses of the Relief-F algorithm is set to $k = 10$.

4.1.3.1 Results of the Attribute Ranking and Selection Before Admission

Tables B.2 and B.4 show the top three attributes from the data that is available before admission obtained with the IG and Relief-F approach, respectively. Both attribute rankings show that attributes which are related to "admission diagnosis 1" (among others the "category code of admission diagnosis 1") are among the top three ranks. This result is not surprising because "diagnosis-related" groups are classified. The "department of admission" also influences the DRG, as discovered by both algorithms. Moreover, for most of the datasets, the DRG grouper-related attributes (e.g. "DRG calculated by using the DRG grouper at 1st contact") are highly relevant which is, however, not true for datasets 3, 6, 9 and 12. One explanation for this is that the artificially generated attribute "DRG calculated by using the DRG grouper" is highly inaccurate since for those four datasets no admission diagnosis codes are available (see Table 4.2) and therefore the DRG grouper cannot classify the DRG accurately. Also, one can observe that the attribute "5" (see datasets 3, 6 and 9 in the Relief-F ranking from Table B.4) is relevant while "5" denotes the first digit of a surgical procedure code. Accordingly, in the case of dataset 3, 6 and 9 this attribute can be considered more relevant than the DRG calculated by using the DRG grouper.

Next, the influence of IG and Relief-F attribute ranking on the two Markov blanket attribute selection techniques and the wrapper subset evaluation is examined. For the Markov blanket attribute selection the χ^2-test with 0.05 % confidence level

Table 4.5 Original number of attributes and number of selected attributes for the different attribute selection techniques with attributes ranked by IG (Relief-F) before admission

Dataset	Original #attributes	Markov blanket			
		GS	IA	GSWL	IAWL
1	2,049	1 (1)	1 (1)	161 (161)	161 (161)
2	2,034	1 (1)	1 (1)	156 (156)	156 (156)
3	2,031	1 (1)	1 (1)	155 (155)	155 (155)
4	1,678	1 (1)	1 (1)	152 (152)	152 (152)
5	1,663	1 (1)	1 (1)	147 (147)	147 (147)
6	1,660	1 (1)	1 (1)	146 (146)	146 (146)
7	1,309	1 (1)	1 (1)	139 (139)	139 (139)
8	1,294	1 (1)	1 (1)	134 (134)	134 (134)
9	1,291	1 (1)	1 (1)	133 (133)	133 (133)
10	251	1 (1)	1 (1)	10 (10)	10 (10)
11	236	1 (1)	1 (1)	5 (5)	5 (5)
12	233	1 (1)	1 (1)	4 (4)	4 (4)

is employed. The influence of whitelisting, i.e., fixing arcs in the Markov blanket DAG when attributes have a functional relationship with the DRG is evaluated. For this purpose, the GS algorithm with whitelisting (GSWL) and the IA algorithm with whitelisting (IAWL) are compared. The original number of attributes and the number of selected attributes by employing the different approaches are shown in Table 4.5 which reveals that the Markov blanket attribute selection without whitelisting, see columns GS and IA, selects for each dataset only one attribute, no matter whether attributes are ranked by IG or Relief-F or which algorithm is employed.

However, a more detailed evaluation to find out which attribute is actually selected reveals that there exist differences whether IG or Relief-F is used prior to attribute selection: For the datasets where attributes are ranked by IG, the selected attribute for datasets 1, 2, 4 and 5 is "DRG calculated by using the DRG grouper at 1st contact". For datasets 3, 6, 9 and 12 it is "department documented at 1st contact" and for datasets 7, 8, 10 and 11 it is "admission diagnosis 1". On the contrary, for the datasets where attributes are ranked by Relief-F, the selected attribute for datasets 1 and 2 is "first three characters of the DRG calculated by using the DRG grouper at 1st contact" while for datasets 3–12 it is "department documented at 1st contact". One explanation that only these attributes are in the Markov blanket is because, based on conditional independence, these three types of strongly relevant attributes (DRG, diagnoses and department) shield the actual DRG from other attributes.

Since in practice not only the attribute "admission diagnosis 1" but also other admission diagnoses, gender and age are connected to DRG by decision rules (see Fig. 1.1) the Markov blanket search leads to a too small set of attributes. Therefore, it was decided to evaluate the impact of whitelisting on the Markov blanket search strategy. If applicable, the DRG classified by the DRG grouper, category codes of each admission diagnosis, first three-digits of procedure codes, age, gender and weight in the case of newborns are inserted into a whitelist of

Table 4.6 Number of
selected attributes for the
wrapper attribute selection
and CFS with attributes
ranked by IG (Relief-F)
before admission

Dataset	Wrapper		CFS
	NB	PA	
1	7 (6)	13 (14)	44
2	6 (6)	12 (10)	45
3	35 (30)	38 (36)	65
4	4 (4)	6 (9)	59
5	4 (4)	7 (7)	62
6	22 (24)	43 (37)	78
7	9 (12)	15 (18)	41
8	11 (11)	18 (17)	44
9	21 (20)	38 (36)	47
10	9 (13)	15 (20)	20
11	14 (13)	21 (28)	20
12	32 (26)	20 (30)	37

tuples such that each of these attributes is connected with the class DRG by an
arc. The reason to do so is because these attributes are in a functional relation to
DRG. Furthermore, an arc from the department-attribute to the DRG is added into
the whitelist since this attribute is discovered by the Markov blanket search without
whitelisting. The number of selected attributes are shown in Table 4.5, too. One
can observe that there are no differences in the number of selected attributes when
the datasets are filtered by using IG or Relief-F attribute ranking methods prior to
Markov blanket attribute selection.

For the wrapper approach, accuracy is employed as an evaluation measure.
However, due to the computational time of this approach, the focus is exclusively on
the first 50 attributes ranked by IG or Relief-F. Moreover, the classification schemes
naive Bayes (NB) and probability averaging (PA) are compared within the wrapper
approach. The reason to use these two approaches is because the cross-validation
of NB is performed relatively fast. Moreover, the PA approach is favored over the
voting approach because the PA approach combines a lower number of classifiers
and therefore the cross-validation process to discover attribute subsets is assumed
to be faster. The results of the wrapper approach as well as the CFS are shown in
Table 4.6. The number of attributes selected by CFS is in all except two cases more
than the attributes selected by the wrappers. The NB wrapper approach selects in
most of the cases less attributes than the PA wrapper approach. One explanation
for this is that the probability averaging approach combines different classification
methods while each of these can potentially combine more attributes in order to
increase accuracy.

4.1.3.2 Results of the Attribute Ranking and Selection at Admission

Tables B.3 and B.5 show the top three attributes from the data that is available at
admission obtained with the IG and Relief-F approach, respectively. In both attribute

Table 4.7 Original number of attributes and number of selected attributes for the different attribute selection techniques with attributes ranked by IG (Relief-F) at admission

Dataset	Original #attributes	Markov blanket			
		GS	IA	GSWL	IAWL
13	2,908	1 (1)	1 (1)	146 (146)	146 (146)
14	2,393	1 (1)	1 (1)	134 (134)	134 (134)
15	1,952	1 (1)	1 (1)	121 (121)	121 (121)
16	265	1 (1)	1 (1)	12 (12)	12 (12)

Table 4.8 Number of selected attributes for the wrapper attribute selection and CFS with attributes ranked by IG (Relief-F) at admission

Dataset	Wrapper		CFS
	NB	PA	
13	11 (14)	24 (29)	76
14	9 (12)	28 (31)	109
15	12 (15)	19 (16)	53
16	9 (12)	31 (20)	11

rankings, at least one DRG grouper-related attribute is among the top three ranks. For datasets 14–16, the IG attribute ranking gives the attribute "admission diagnosis 1" the highest rank. In contrast, the results of the Relief-F attribute ranking reveal that no admission diagnosis-related attribute is among the top three ranks. Instead, the DRG grouper-related attributes, e.g., "MDC of the DRG calculated by using the DRG grouper at admission" are among the top three ranked attributes.

In order to examine the influence of IG and Relief-F attribute ranking on the two Markov blanket attribute selection techniques and the wrapper subset evaluation at admission, a 10 % sample stratified by DRG is employed for each dataset. This means that the probability distribution of DRGs in the sample is equal to the one of the original dataset. The results are shown in Table 4.7. Similar to the results obtained by GS and IA before admission, for the group of IG ranked attributes, the selected attribute for dataset 13 is "DRG calculated by using the DRG grouper at 1st contact" and for datasets 14–16 it is "admission diagnosis 1". For the group of Relief-F ranked attributes, the selected attribute for dataset 13 is "DRG calculated by using the DRG grouper at admission" and for datasets 14–16 it is "MDC of the DRG calculated by using the DRG grouper at admission".

Now, looking at the wrapper and the CFS approach (see Table 4.8), the PA wrapper approach leads, similar to the results before admission, to a larger number of selected attributes as compared to the NB wrapper.

4.1.4 Evaluation Techniques for the Classification Part

All classifiers and the DRG grouper are assessed using the same performance indicators. The overall performance is measured in terms of classification accuracy (proportion of correctly classified DRGs) as well as classification accuracy within each of five different major diagnostic categories (MDCs) relevant before admission and eight MDCs relevant at admission. Each of the MDCs represents broad categories of diagnoses (e.g. respiratory, gastrointestinal). For a selection of eight frequently occurring DRGs such as "esophagitis", the true positive rate and false positive rate are measured. As described in Sect. 4.1.10, it is evaluated, how well each classifier predicts the expected revenue for each inpatient. The DRG's base revenue rate is used, and the mean absolute difference between true and predicted revenue is measured. Each performance indicator is measured using 10-fold cross-validation.

Another quality measure that is employed in this experimental study is the learning curve of each classifier. Learning curves show the accuracy of a classifier as a function of the size of the training set (see Perlich et al. [162]). In order to obtain a learning curve for the classifiers, a sample is drawn from the data which is stratified by DRG. The classifiers are trained and tested on this small dataset using 10-fold cross-validation. Afterwards, the classification accuracy is stored as a function of the sample size. These steps (sampling and cross-validation) are repeated by increasing the sample size until it is equal to the size of the original dataset.

4.1.5 Computation Times

All computations were performed on a 3.16 GHz PC (Intel Core2 Duo E8500) with 8 GB RAM, running Windows 7 64 bit operating system. For the Markov blanket searches, the "bnlearn" package (see Scutari [199]) is employed. For carrying out the attribute ranking, the CFS and the classification tasks, the Java-based Weka machine learning application programming interface from Witten and Frank [233] was employed. In order to incorporate the DRG grouper-related probability averaging approach, the package was extended in this dissertation.

4.1.5.1 Computation Times for the Attribute Ranking, Selection and Classification Before Admission

The computation times of the attribute ranking and selection algorithms employed before admission are reported in Tables 4.9–4.11 while the computation times for generating the attribute rankings were excluded from the four computation times of the Markov blanket search and the wrapper approach.

Comparing the attribute ranking techniques (see Table 4.9), Relief-F requires considerably more computation time than IG. The observation that IG is faster than Relief-F is not surprising because the computational complexity of IG is relatively low as compared to the one of Relief-F, for which the k-nearest hits and k-nearest misses must be selected for each sampled instance. Furthermore, Markov blanket attribute selection with whitelisting requires considerably more computation time

Table 4.9 Run time (s) for generating the attribute rankings before admission

Dataset	Attribute ranking	
	IG	Relief-F
1	**0.89**	18.58
2	**0.59**	16.57
3	**0.41**	14.26
4	**0.39**	16.68
5	**0.34**	14.65
6	**0.30**	12.40
7	**0.37**	17.05
8	**0.27**	12.92
9	**0.22**	10.87
10	**0.11**	12.56
11	**0.08**	10.55
12	**0.05**	8.33
Avg.	**0.34**	13.79

Table 4.10 Run time (s) for the Markov blanket attribute selection before admission

Dataset	IG				Relief-F			
	GS	IA	GSWL	IAWL	GS	IA	GSWL	IAWL
1	3.88	8.02	39.95	39.02	**3.81**	7.56	41.12	39.95
2	7.33	**6.09**	32.56	31.62	6.69	6.55	34.79	33.60
3	2.33	**2.2**	14.63	14.6	2.68	2.64	17.45	17.58
4	2.01	**1.97**	32.01	31.45	2.34	2.29	34.40	33.30
5	1.91	**1.79**	25.38	24.22	2.14	2.11	27.66	26.55
6	**1.66**	1.68	8.46	8.42	1.91	2.01	11.21	11.22
7	**1.5**	1.59	24.18	23.46	1.64	1.7	26.63	25.52
8	**1.31**	1.41	18.11	16.99	1.54	1.56	20.24	18.92
9	**1.27**	**1.27**	5.01	5.01	1.46	1.43	6.89	6.88
10	0.52	**0.5**	9.61	8.58	0.52	0.55	9.22	8.50
11	**0.37**	0.48	3.95	4.05	**0.37**	0.39	3.91	4.07
12	0.38	**0.25**	0.42	0.41	0.3	0.28	0.39	0.44
Avg.	**2.04**	2.27	17.86	17.32	2.12	2.42	19.49	18.88

than the one without whitelisting (see Table 4.10). Though, the figures reveal no significant differences in computation times between the Markov blanket attribute selection approaches using different rankings. The computation times for CFS is between the run time of IG and Relief-F. The run times for the wrapper approaches (see Table 4.11) are substantially higher than the ones of all other ranking or selection techniques. This is not surprising since for the wrapper approach, the classifiers are rebuilt and cross-validation is performed for each attribute evaluation step. Furthermore, the figures reveal that for the wrapper approaches, the Relief-F ranked approaches are most of the times slower than the IG ranked approaches.

The computation times for the classification techniques without attribute selection are shown in Table 4.12 and include the time for 10-fold cross-validation.

Table 4.11 Run time (s) for the CFS and for the wrapper attribute selection before admission

| Dataset | CFS | Wrapper | | | |
| | | IG | | Relief-F | |
		NB	PA	NB	PA
1	8.44	**522.48**	3, 609.38	541.80	4, 217.89
2	9.16	**472.99**	4, 845.09	509.12	4, 277.59
3	9.24	**3, 217.57**	7, 818.02	4, 847.70	9, 175.77
4	5.49	**337.35**	3, 301.92	365.70	3, 848.47
5	5.12	**348.86**	2, 792.67	362.26	2, 787.44
6	7.19	**1, 792.62**	8, 129.05	4, 096.42	9, 093.80
7	4.34	**762.98**	12, 542.53	1, 264.63	11, 709.09
8	3.71	**953.20**	12, 595.58	1, 010.83	11, 947.53
9	5.41	**1, 600.96**	7, 841.69	3, 624.66	8, 921.97
10	0.81	**672.82**	15, 425.09	1, 493.73	20, 710.98
11	0.59	1, 121.74	17, 070.54	**1, 121.64**	23, 585.11
12	0.83	**2, 724.43**	3, 375.44	4, 519.56	7, 352.71
Avg.	5.03	**1, 210.67**	8, 278.92	1, 979.84	9, 802.36

Table 4.12 Run time (s) for the classification techniques without attribute selection before admission

Dataset	Rule	NB	BN	Tree	Vote	PA
1	**6.99**	219.74	493.68	49.66	778.81	524.36
2	**6.29**	205.50	627.87	50.20	876.11	723.14
3	**5.93**	189.56	513.10	396.30	1,181.54	1,004.12
4	**5.30**	165.13	256.91	45.63	601.05	423.69
5	**4.93**	156.94	262.56	39.81	576.29	426.17
6	**4.70**	146.72	243.04	280.63	801.03	644.09
7	**3.96**	119.50	214.56	203.33	620.05	494.64
8	**3.76**	108.17	217.07	178.95	580.90	461.97
9	**3.48**	99.71	183.54	174.72	560.52	451.06
10	**0.86**	22.12	39.32	119.48	202.95	177.28
11	**0.76**	19.38	34.34	83.93	156.42	135.11
12	**0.66**	17.32	31.94	24.13	91.64	71.92
Avg.	**3.97**	122.48	259.83	137.23	585.61	461.46

Not surprisingly, the computational time of the voting approach is roughly equal to the sum of the computation times of the NB, BN and classification tree methods. Since BN, classification trees and the DRG grouper are employed as the set of classifiers within the PA approach instead of using BN, NB, rules and classification trees within the voting approach, the computation time of the PA approach is approximately equal to the run time for the voting approach minus the computation time for the NB and the decision rule approach.

Table 4.13 Run time (s) for generating the attribute rankings at admission

Dataset	IG	Relief-F
13	**2.67**	430.41
14	**2.32**	376.68
15	**1.86**	356.71
16	**0.66**	327.15
Avg.	**1.88**	372.74

Table 4.14 Run time (s) for generating the Markov blanket attribute selection at admission

	IG				Relief-F			
Dataset	GS	IA	GSWL	IAWL	GS	IA	GSWL	IAWL
13	6.22	5.69	14.60	14.46	4.75	**4.71**	15.45	15.00
14	1.49	**1.35**	11.31	11.53	1.51	1.45	12.20	12.38
15	1.24	**1.1**	9.22	9.03	1.32	1.18	10.23	9.81
16	**0.66**	0.69	5.15	5.08	0.82	0.75	5.05	5.09
Avg.	2.40	2.21	10.07	10.03	2.10	**2.02**	10.73	10.57

Table 4.15 Run time (s) for the CFS and for the wrapper attribute selection at admission

		Wrapper			
		IG		Relief-F	
Dataset	CFS	NB	PA	NB	PA
13	104.37	**7,323.68**	76, 221.00	25,011.80	103, 261.68
14	85.22	**5,874.40**	91, 421.20	29,563.98	102, 045.79
15	61.96	**9,351.36**	65, 971.31	36,267.89	57, 149.17
16	8.39	**5,718.79**	115, 569.92	30,311.59	87, 626.10
Avg.	64.99	**7,067.06**	87, 295.86	30,288.82	87, 520.69

4.1.5.2   Computation Times for the Attribute Ranking, Selection and Classification at Admission

The computation times for the attribute ranking and selection algorithms employed at admission are reported in Tables 4.13–4.15 while, again, the computation times for generating the attribute rankings are excluded from the four computation times of the Markov blanket search and the wrapper approach. The tables reveal that the computational times for generating the attribute rankings at admission (see Table 4.13) are considerably higher than the computational times for generating the attribute rankings before admission (see Table 4.9). One reason for this is that the datasets are larger at admission, compared to the datasets before admission in which elective patients are considered only and accordingly, the number of attributes and instances are less.

Similar to the observations before admission, the computational time for the CFS is between IG and Relief-F (see Tables 4.13 and 4.15). The run times for the wrapper approaches applied to the data available at admission (see Table 4.15)

Table 4.16 Run time (s) for the classification techniques without attribute selection at admission

Dataset	Rule	NB	BN	Tree	Vote	PA
13	**111.48**	2, 281.32	6, 234.92	1, 649.05	9, 604.11	9, 614.42
14	**109.12**	1, 870.29	3, 298.93	948.98	7, 454.78	7, 319.35
15	**88.42**	1, 474.39	2, 198.28	461.34	6, 599.47	6, 097.72
16	**13.20**	210.32	314.09	247.87	939.73	712.37
Avg.	**80.56**	1, 459.08	3, 011.56	826.81	6, 149.52	5, 935.97

are substantially larger than the ones for the data available before admission (see Table 4.11).

The computational times for the classification techniques without attribute selection at admission are shown in Table 4.16 and include the time for 10-fold cross-validation as well. The table reveals that, compared to the classification before admission, computation times are also higher.

4.1.6   Parameter Optimization for the Classification Tree

In order to tune the classification accuracy of the decision tree approach, a two-stage parameter optimization was performed which is outlined in the following.

4.1.6.1   Parameter Optimization Before Admission

For the first-stage parameter optimization, all attributes are considered, i.e., before employing any attribute selection technique. The minimum number of instances per leaf (MI) is varied within the interval [1, 100], employing a step size of 5. The confidence factor (CF) is varied using the following values: $0.001, 0.005, 0.01, 0.05,$ 0.1 and 0.5, and the parameter combination which results in the maximum accuracy is selected. Then, after attribute selection, a second-stage parameter optimization for the decision tree approach is performed by choosing the same interval and step size for MI and the same set of values for CF as for the first-stage parameter optimization. The parameter optimization results for each dataset before and after attribute selection are shown in Tables 4.17 and 4.18. The tables reveal that, before attribute selection, for datasets 3, 6, 9 and 12 low CF values (CF = 0.005) and low MI values (MI = 1) are best.

One explanation for this is that for these datasets only free-text information about admission diagnoses is available and, because of the pruning strategy, even a small number of instances per leaf can substantially increase classification accuracy. The decision to prune the tree is then controlled using a low CF.

Table 4.17 Optimal parameter values for the decision tree learner without attribute selection and after Markov blanket attribute selection or CFS before admission

| | Before | | After attribute selection | | | |
| | | | MB | | CFS | |
Dataset	CF	MI	CF	MI	CF	MI
1	0.05	11	0.001	6	0.001	1
2	0.5	11	0.001	6	0.001	1
3	0.005	1	0.1	1	0.005	1
4	0.5	11	0.001	1	0.05	1
5	0.001	11	0.001	6	0.5	1
6	0.005	1	0.005	1	0.01	1
7	0.01	1	0.005	1	0.5	1
8	0.01	1	0.1	1	0.5	1
9	0.005	1	0.001	1	0.05	1
10	0.05	1	0.1	1	0.5	1
11	0.01	1	0.1	1	0.5	1
12	0.005	1	0.1	11	0.01	1

Table 4.18 Optimal parameter values for the decision tree learner after wrapper attribute selection before admission

| | NB Wrapper | | | | PA Wrapper | | | |
| | IG | | Relief-F | | IG | | Relief-F | |
Dataset	CF	MI	CF	MI	CF	MI	CF	MI
1	0.5	1	0.001	6	0.001	6	0.001	6
2	0.001	6	0.001	6	0.01	1	0.001	6
3	0.005	1	0.005	1	0.05	6	0.005	1
4	0.5	1	0.5	1	0.1	1	0.05	1
5	0.001	6	0.001	6	0.05	1	0.05	1
6	0.1	1	0.01	1	0.005	1	0.05	6
7	0.1	1	0.1	1	0.1	1	0.5	1
8	0.1	1	0.1	1	0.05	1	0.05	1
9	0.005	6	0.01	6	0.005	1	0.01	1
10	0.1	1	0.05	1	0.5	1	0.1	1
11	0.5	1	0.1	1	0.1	1	0.05	1
12	0.01	1	0.001	1	0.5	1	0.001	1

4.1.6.2   Parameter Optimization at Admission

For the datasets that are available at admission, the procedure is similar to the one for the datasets available before admission. However, MI is varied within the interval [10, 100], employing the same step size of 5. The results for each dataset are shown in Tables 4.19 and 4.20. The tables reveal that, in comparison to the datasets before admission, the optimal MI is always 10 while a CF of 0.5 is preferred in most of the cases.

Table 4.19 Optimal parameter values for the decision tree learner without attribute selection and after Markov blanket attribute selection or CFS at admission

| | Before | | After attribute selection | | | |
| | | | MB | | CFS | |
Dataset	CF	MI	CF	MI	CF	MI
13	0.5	10	0.5	10	0.5	10
14	0.1	10	0.5	15	0.5	10
15	0.1	10	0.5	10	0.5	10
16	0.5	10	0.5	10	0.1	10

Table 4.20 Optimal parameter values for the decision tree learner after wrapper attribute selection at admission

| | NB Wrapper | | | | PA Wrapper | | | |
| | IG | | Relief-F | | IG | | Relief-F | |
Dataset	CF	MI	CF	MI	CF	MI	CF	MI
13	0.5	10	0.5	10	0.1	10	0.5	10
14	0.5	10	0.5	10	0.5	10	0.1	10
15	0.5	10	0.5	10	0.5	10	0.5	10
16	0.5	10	0.5	10	0.1	10	0.5	10

4.1.7   Results of the Classification Techniques

Now, the performance of the different classifiers and the DRG grouper with and without attribute selection are compared.

4.1.7.1   Results of the Classification Techniques Before Admission

The large-sample results (10-fold cross validation accuracy for each dataset) before attribute selection and before admission are given in Table 4.21 which reveal that the probability averaging approach (PA) which combines machine learning techniques with the DRG grouper always outperforms the current approach employed in the hospital (DRG grouper). Moreover, compared to the other machine learning approaches, the PA approach can outperform them in 6 out of the 12 datasets. None of the approaches BN, NB, decision rules, classification trees, or voting outperforms the current approach of the hospital for all datasets. Remarkably, the NB approach has always a poor accuracy with a maximum of 44.4% (see dataset 11) and obtains a lower average performance as compared to the DRG grouper. Furthermore, the trivial baseline classifier (decision rules) outperforms the DRG grouper for datasets 3, 6 and 9–12.

In what follows, the classification results with attribute selection before admission are presented. Tables 4.22a, b show the results for the Markov blanket attribute selection with whitelisting and the CFS.

Table 4.21 Overall accuracy (%) of the different classification techniques before attribute selection and before admission

Dataset	BN	DRG grouper	PA	NB	Rules	Tree	Vote
1	70.0	77.9	**78.7**	35.5	75.8	75.8	75.9
2	70.2	77.2	**77.9**	37.4	75.2	75.3	75.5
3	55.9	0.8	58.3	30.5	20.1	**62.1**	52.1
4	66.4	71.9	**72.8**	35.0	70.2	70.2	70.4
5	66.5	71.3	**72.0**	38.2	69.7	69.7	69.9
6	52.0	0.8	53.5	31.1	20.1	**56.5**	48.4
7	59.9	52.1	**63.4**	33.7	45.2	60.1	58.6
8	59.7	51.9	**63.3**	36.8	45.2	60.8	59.0
9	44.8	0.7	43.5	27.3	20.1	**48.2**	41.3
10	52.3	18.3	52.5	39.5	45.2	52.9	**54.2**
11	51.5	18.3	52.3	44.4	45.2	52.7	**53.6**
12	31.1	0.1	28.3	33.4	20.1	**38.7**	35.3
Avg.	56.7	36.8		59.7	35.2	46.0	**60.3**	57.9

The tables reveal that in most of the cases, Markov blanket attribute selection yields higher classification accuracies than attribute selection by employing CFS. Furthermore, when comparing the results before attribute selection (see Table 4.21) with the results after attribute selection using MB or CFS (see Table 4.22), the maximum achieved overall accuracy can be increased for datasets 1, 2, 4 and 5. Another observation from the comparison of the results before and after attribute selection is that Markov blanket attribute selection can improve classification accuracy for the NB approach in 10 of the 12 datasets. Furthermore, attribute selection has no impact for the decision rule approach.

The results of the NB wrapper approach employed before admission and shown in Table 4.23a reveal that when using this approach, searching within the first 50 attributes ranked by IG or Relief-F is sufficient to substantially improve the accuracy of the NB classifier as compared to the results before attribute selection (see Table 4.21).

The results for the PA wrapper attribute selection are shown in Tables 4.24a, b which reveal that although the PA wrapper approach does not search within the entire set of attributes, it can increase classification accuracy significantly as compared to the results of the DRG grouper (see Table 4.21) while significance tests were performed using a t-test for paired observations on a 5 % confidence level. However, when comparing the results of the PA classifier before attribute selection (see Table 4.21) with the ones of the PA classifier after PA wrapper attribute selection (see Table 4.24), one can observe that for some datasets, classification accuracy does not improve which is in particular true for datasets that contain free-text attributes (e.g., datasets 3, 6, 9 and 12). One explanation for this is that the PA wrapper searches within a limited set of 50 attributes ranked by IG or Relief-F.

Table 4.22 Overall accuracy (%) of the BN, PA and NB (a) as well as the decision rules, tree and voting classification techniques (b) after Markov blanket (CFS) attribute selection before admission

(a)

Dataset	BN	PA	NB
1	71.7 (72.2)	79.1 (**79.2**)	49.7 (57.3)
2	72.1 (62.0)	**78.5** (78.0)	56.0 (57.3)
3	50.0 (36.8)	49.4 (29.3)	45.2 (38.2)
4	67.5 (70.0)	**73.3** (72.6)	46.2 (60.1)
5	67.3 (69.4)	**72.2** (71.9)	52.9 (59.5)
6	46.6 (31.7)	41.1 (22.9)	41.1 (32.7)
7	59.9 (61.2)	62.1 (**63.2**)	40.4 (54.9)
8	60.5 (61.2)	61.3 (**62.9**)	46.7 (54.8)
9	39.2 (25.7)	29.7 (15.8)	34.7 (29.7)
10	52.1 (52.2)	49.7 (51.1)	38.8 (49.0)
11	51.3 (52.3)	47.8 (51.1)	45.8 (49.0)
12	21.6 (23.0)	8.8 (11.2)	26.9 (26.2)
Avg.	55.0 (51.5)	54.4 (50.8)	43.7 (47.4)

(b)

Dataset	Rules	Tree	Vote
1	75.8 (75.8)	76.6 (76.8)	76.6 (76.6)
2	75.2 (75.2)	76.0 (76.1)	76.2 (74.4)
3	20.1 (20.1)	**54.5** (40.6)	50.4 (39.1)
4	70.2 (70.2)	70.6 (70.4)	71.2 (70.8)
5	69.7 (69.7)	70.0 (70.0)	70.5 (70.3)
6	20.1 (20.1)	**51.8** (36.6)	46.7 (34.6)
7	45.2 (45.2)	58.8 (60.8)	59.3 (60.4)
8	45.2 (45.2)	58.7 (60.7)	59.8 (60.4)
9	20.1 (20.1)	**42.5** (29.9)	39.5 (29.7)
10	45.2 (45.2)	51.8 (52.9)	**53.2** (52.8)
11	45.2 (45.2)	51.0 (**53.2**)	51.5 (52.8)
12	20.1 (20.1)	**27.6** (26.7)	25.3 (26.9)
Avg.	46.0 (46.0)	**57.5** (54.5)	56.7 (54.1)

4.1.7.2   Results of the Classification Techniques at Admission

The results before attribute selection and at admission are given in Table 4.25. Similar to the classification before admission, the trivial baseline classifier (decision rules) outperforms the DRG grouper for datasets 13, 14 and 16. Moreover, the PA approach, decision trees and voting outperforms the DRG grouper for each of the four datasets. Now, when Markov blanket attribute selection with whitelisting and CFS are employed (see Table 4.26a, b) the Markov blanket attribute selection can only improve the maximum obtained accuracy for dataset 14, as compared to the results obtained without attribute selection (see Table 4.25).

Table 4.23 Overall accuracy (%) of the BN, PA and NB (a) as well as the decision rules, tree and voting classification techniques (b) after naive Bayes wrapper attribute selection with IG (Relief-F) ranking before admission

(a)

Dataset	BN	PA	NB
1	75.6 (75.9)	78.0 **(78.2)**	71.0 (71.0)
2	75.1 (75.1)	**77.6 (77.6)**	70.8 (70.8)
3	39.3 (39.9)	29.3 (31.5)	41.2 (44.3)
4	70.1 (70.1)	**72.2 (72.2)**	65.7 (65.7)
5	69.1 (69.1)	**71.6 (71.6)**	65.6 (65.6)
6	37.0 (34.4)	20.1 (26.4)	37.1 **(41.7)**
7	60.3 (60.7)	**62.4** (62.2)	58.6 (58.8)
8	60.6 (60.6)	**62.1** (62.0)	58.8 (58.8)
9	34.7 (34.0)	18.8 (22.3)	35.5 **(39.0)**
10	51.4 (51.8)	50.8 (50.9)	50.4 (51.0)
11	51.9 (52.5)	51.0 (50.9)	50.9 (51.1)
12	32.0 (32.4)	17.6 (20.0)	34.2 **(37.8)**
Avg.	54.7 (54.7)	50.9 (52.1)	53.3 (54.6)

(b)

Dataset	Rules	Tree	Vote
1	75.8 (75.8)	76.0 (75.8)	76.1 (76.0)
2	75.2 (75.2)	75.2 (75.2)	75.3 (75.3)
3	20.1 (20.1)	41.6 **(45.2)**	41.5 (44.0)
4	70.2 (70.2)	70.5 (70.5)	70.6 (70.6)
5	69.7 (69.7)	69.7 (69.7)	69.8 (69.8)
6	20.1 (20.1)	37.6 (41.5)	37.4 (39.8)
7	45.2 (45.2)	60.0 (60.0)	60.6 (60.7)
8	45.2 (45.2)	59.9 (59.9)	60.8 (60.8)
9	20.1 (20.1)	35.3 (39.0)	35.6 (38.3)
10	45.2 (45.2)	52.2 (52.5)	52.8 **(53.7)**
11	45.2 (45.2)	52.3 (52.6)	53.4 **(53.6)**
12	20.1 (20.1)	33.1 (35.9)	33.8 (36.5)
Avg.	46.0 (46.0)	55.3 (56.5)	55.6 **(56.6)**

More specifically, using this attribute selection technique, the classification accuracies for BN and decision trees can be improved for all datasets. In contrast, the classification accuracy of NB can be improved for all datasets when using CFS attribute selection.

The results of the NB wrapper approach employed at admission (see Table 4.27a) reveal that, similar to the results before admission (see Table 4.23a), the classification accuracy of the NB approach is boosted when using the corresponding wrapper.

The results for the PA wrapper attribute selection are shown in Table 4.28a, b which reveal that, compared to the results without attribute selection, overall classification accuracy can be improved only slightly when using the PA wrapper for datasets 14–16.

Table 4.24 Overall accuracy (%) of the BN, PA and NB (a) as well as the decision rules, tree and voting classification techniques (b) after PA wrapper attribute selection with IG (Relief-F) ranking before admission

(a)

Dataset	BN	PA	NB
1	70.9 (72.8)	79.4 (**79.5**[a])	56.1 (60.0)
2	73.3 (73.5)	**78.9** (**78.9**[a])	65.5 (65.6)
3	38.8 (38.7)	30.5 (34.1)	40.9 (43.8)
4	66.5 (69.4)	73.0 (**73.2**[a])	51.4 (61.3)
5	68.9 (68.9)	**72.4** (**72.4**[a])	62.5 (62.5)
6	32.9 (37.1)	27.0 (31.7)	36.3 (41.2)
7	58.7 (59.3)	63.3 (**63.6**[a])	50.3 (52.9)
8	60.7 (60.6)	**63.3** (**63.3**[a])	57.6 (57.3)
9	32.0 (33.2)	24.1 (26.7)	34.8 (38.0)
10	53.7 (53.2)	52.9 (53.4[a])	47.3 (48.1)
11	53.0 (52.7)	52.1 (52.6[a])	49.7 (49.7)
12	30.1 (32.1)	16.8 (23.1)	30.0 (**37.3**)
Avg.	53.3 (54.3)	52.8 (54.4)	48.5 (51.5)

(b)

Dataset	Rules	Tree	Vote
1	75.8 (75.8)	76.4 (76.3)	76.1 (76.3)
2	75.2 (75.2)	76.0 (76.0)	76.2 (76.0)
3	20.1 (20.1)	41.6 (**45.4**)	41.4 (43.3)
4	70.2 (70.2)	70.8 (70.8)	70.6 (70.9)
5	69.7 (69.7)	70.5 (70.5)	70.1 (70.1)
6	20.1 (20.1)	37.9 (**44.0**)	37.0 (41.6)
7	45.2 (45.2)	59.9 (60.1)	58.5 (59.6)
8	45.2 (45.2)	60.0 (59.9)	60.6 (60.5)
9	20.1 (20.1)	35.5 (**39.3**)	35.6 (38.0)
10	45.2 (45.2)	53.7 (53.5)	54.4 (**54.5**)
11	45.2 (45.2)	52.7 (52.9)	53.7 (**54.4**)
12	20.1 (20.1)	30.0 (36.1)	30.2 (36.6)
Avg.	46.0 (46.0)	55.4 (**57.1**)	55.4 (56.8)

[a] Significant improvement as compared to the DRG grouper, see Table 4.21

Table 4.25 Overall accuracy (%) of the different classification techniques before attribute selection and at admission

Dataset	BN	DRG Grouper	PA	NB	Rules	Tree	Vote
13	60.8	60.8	**65.5**	32.1	61.7	63.7	63.8
14	56.5	56.6	**59.7**	32.7	57.3	58.4	58.6
15	53.2	49.8	**55.2**	32.5	45.2	54.4	53.8
16	49.1	37.1	49.7	39.7	45.2	49.3	**50.4**
Avg.	54.9	51.1	**57.5**	34.3	52.4	56.5	56.7

Table 4.26 Overall accuracy (%) of the BN, PA and NB (a) as well as the decision rules, tree and voting classification techniques (b) after Markov blanket (CFS) attribute selection at admission

(a)

Dataset	BN	PA	NB
13	62.5 (63.5)	**65.0** (63.5)	43.9 (57.4)
14	58.1 (58.4)	**59.9** (58.7)	40.6 (51.9)
15	54.2 (54.3)	54.9 (54.1)	37.4 (51.3)
16	49.7 (49.4)	47.8 (48.0)	36.2 (47.0)
Avg.	56.1 (56.4)	56.9 (56.1)	39.5 (51.9)

(b)

Dataset	Rules	Tree	Vote
13	61.7 (61.7)	64.7 (62.8)	64.6 (63.1)
14	57.3 (57.3)	59.5 (57.9)	59.5 (58.4)
15	45.2 (45.2)	**55.0** (54.1)	54.4 (54.0)
16	45.2 (45.2)	49.7 (48.0)	**50.0** (49.4)
Avg.	52.3 (52.3)	**57.2** (55.7)	57.1 (56.2)

Table 4.27 Overall accuracy (%) of the BN, PA and NB (a) as well as the decision rules, tree and voting classification techniques (b) after naive Bayes wrapper attribute selection with IG (Relief-F) ranking at admission

(a)

Dataset	BN	PA	NB
13	63.4 (63.4)	64.4 (**64.6**)	61.5 (61.7)
14	58.8 (58.7)	59.5 (**59.6**)	57.1 (57.5)
15	54.4 (54.7)	54.9 (54.8)	53.5 (53.9)
16	49.1 (49.2)	48.4 (48.6)	49.0 (49.4)
Avg.	56.4 (56.5)	56.8 (56.9)	55.3 (55.6)

(b)

Dataset	Rules	Tree	Vote
13	61.7 (61.7)	63.5 (63.6)	64.1 (64.3)
14	57.3 (57.3)	58.5 (58.7)	59.2 (59.4)
15	45.2 (45.2)	54.3 (54.4)	54.7 (55.1)
16	45.2 (45.2)	49.1 (49.7)	50.3 (**50.6**)
Avg.	52.3 (52.3)	56.4 (56.6)	57.1 (**57.4**)

4.1.7.3   Learning Curves for the DRG Classification Before and at Admission

In the following, the learning curves of the classifiers are evaluated in order to examine how the number of training cases influences classification accuracy. Datasets 1 and 16 are selected because the first dataset refers to elective patients that contact the hospital before admission assuming that information about all clinical procedures is available. In contrast, the last dataset refers to the current situation at the hospital where at admission, the DRG grouper has only access to those attributes which are available in dataset 16. Attributes are selected based on the PA wrapper approach since this approach achieves highest classification accuracy for

Table 4.28 Overall accuracy (%) of the BN, PA and NB (a) as well as the decision rules, tree and voting classification techniques (b) after PA wrapper attribute selection with IG (Relief-F) ranking at admission

(a)

Dataset	BN	PA	NB
13	60.4 (59.8)	**65.0**[a] (64.9)	46.1 (55.5)
14	56.8 (55.7)	**60.1**[a] (60.0)	48.4 (52.7)
15	54.1 (53.9)	**55.4**[a] **(55.4)**	48.3 (49.9)
16	49.9 (50.7)	49.8[a] (49.8)	41.8 (47.5)
Avg.	55.3 (55.0)	**57.6** (57.5)	46.2 (51.4)

(b)

Dataset	Rules	Tree	Vote
13	61.7 (61.7)	64.6 (64.5)	64.0 (64.1)
14	57.3 (57.3)	59.7 (59.7)	59.4 (59.4)
15	45.2 (45.2)	55.2 (55.3)	54.4 (54.6)
16	45.2 (45.2)	49.9 (50.2)	50.3 (**51.0**)
Avg.	52.3 (52.3)	57.4 (57.4)	57.0 (57.3)

[a] Significant improvement as compared to the DRG grouper, see Table 4.25

these two datasets. Moreover, all six classification methods are compared with the DRG grouper as benchmark. The results for dataset 1 and 16 are shown in Fig. 4.4a, b, respectively. The PA approach, when applied to dataset 1 requires for reaching the accuracy of the DRG grouper approximately 100 samples. However, one can observe that this level slightly decreases with more samples but then increases again by outperforming the DRG grouper as soon as the sample size exceeds 2,351 cases. For dataset 16, the DRG grouper is outperformed by all machine learning approaches when the sample size is more than 2,656 cases.

4.1.8 Investigation on Major Diagnostic Categories

In the DRG systems of many first-world countries, such as the United States and Germany, MDCs are used to group DRGs into 23 different major diagnostic categories on a higher-level. Typically, the DRGs are separated by organ system. From an operations management perspective, the advantage of using MDCs is that they are linked to medical disciplines and therefore are closely linked to medical specialties or clinical care centers.

4.1.8.1 Investigation on Major Diagnostic Categories Before Admission

Now, it will be investigated how classification techniques and the DRG grouper perform with respect to MDCs. For this, dataset 1 will be considered in order to evaluate to what extent machine learning methods can improve the upper bound on

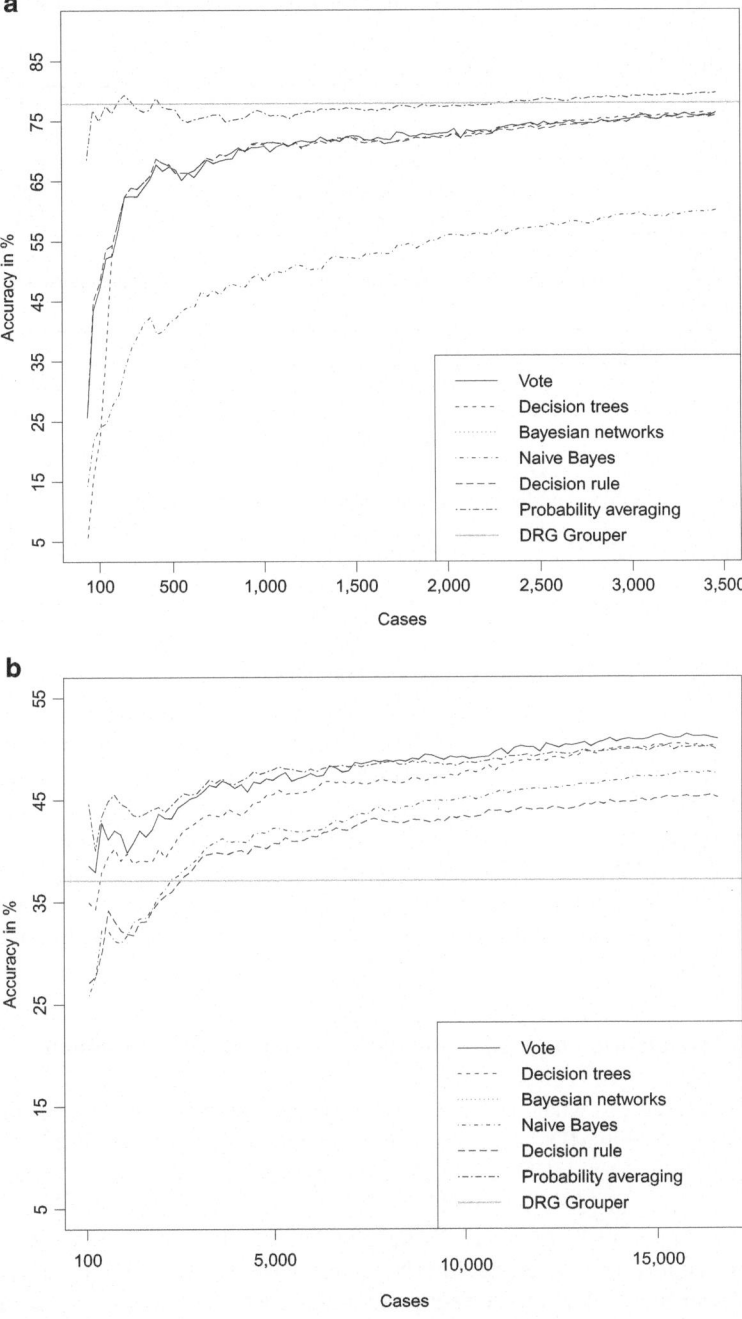

Fig. 4.4 Accuracy as a function of the number of labeled training examples before (**a**) and at admission (**b**)

Table 4.29 The five most frequent major diagnostic categories in the datasets before admission

MDC number	Description	n
4	Respiratory system	101
5	Circulatory system	544
6	Digestive system	334
8	Musculoskeletal system and connective tissue	1,169
11	Kidney and urinary tract	300

Table 4.30 The five most frequent major diagnostic categories in the datasets at admission

MDC number	Description	n
1	Nervous system	1,017
4	Respiratory system	1,121
5	Circulatory system	2,741
6	Digestive system	2,374
8	Musculoskeletal system and connective tissue	2,741
11	Kidney and urinary tract	989
14	Pregnancy and childbirth	914
15	Newborn and other neonates	515

classification accuracy as provided by the DRG grouper, given a maximum amount of available information. Therefore, five of the 23 available categories of which each is represented in the dataset by more than 100 instances are selected, see Table 4.29.

From the results in Sect. 4.1.7, the correctly classified DRGs are matched to the correct MDC. Afterwards, the classification accuracy is computed for each MDC. Figure 4.5 shows the performance of the different classification methods. The figure reveals that for MDC 4 (Respiratory system), the DRG grouper outperforms all machine learning methods. In contrast, for MDCs 5, 6, 8 and 11, the classification accuracy of the machine learning methods is greater than or equal to the one of the DRG grouper.

4.1.8.2 Investigation on Major Diagnostic Categories at Admission

In order to evaluate to what extent machine learning methods can improve classification accuracy in each MDC at admission, the results for dataset 16 will be examined on a more detailed level. Therefore, the MDCs given in Table 4.29 are extended by the MDCs 1, 14 and 15 as provided by Table 4.30. The latter two MDCs usually do not represent patients that contact the hospital before admission. Moreover, each of the eight categories is represented in the dataset by more than 500 instances. From the results in Sect. 4.1.7, the correctly classified DRGs are, again, matched to the correct MDC while Fig. 4.6 shows the performance of the different classification methods employed at admission. The figure reveals that for each MDC, the DRG grouper is outperformed by at least one machine learning method.

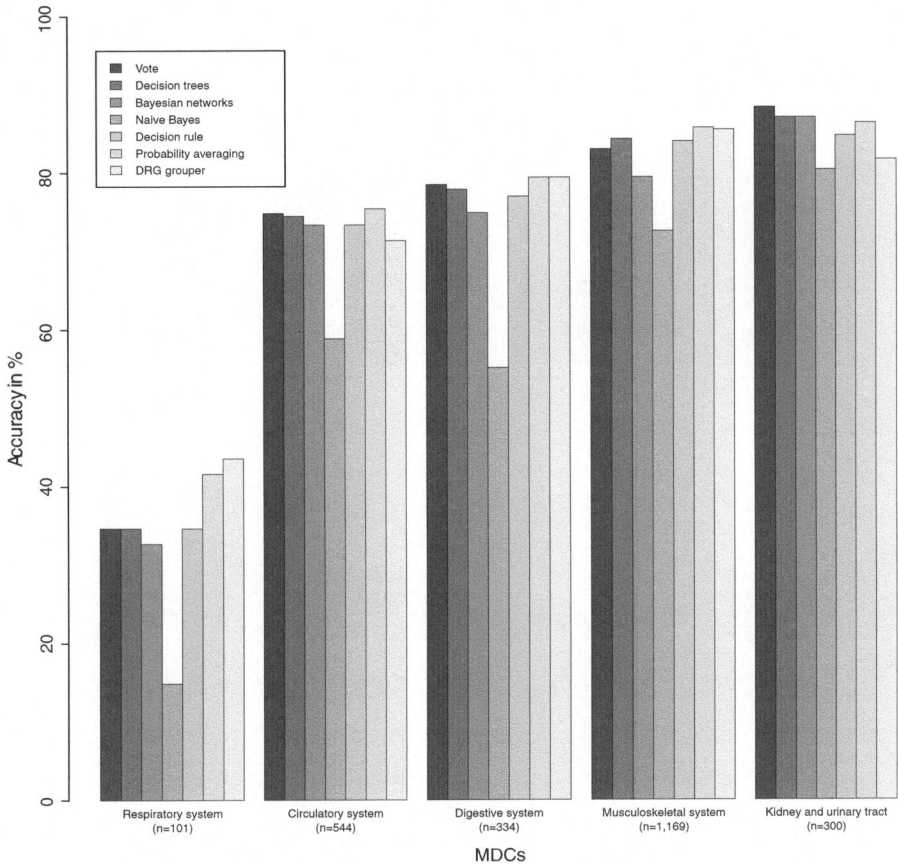

Fig. 4.5 Classification accuracy for different diagnostic categories before admission

4.1.9   Investigation on Selected DRGs

Next, the classification performance of the DRG grouper and the machine learning algorithms are compared at a detailed level on specific, frequently occurring DRGs.

4.1.9.1   Investigation on Selected DRGs Before Admission

For the investigation on selected DRGs before admission, dataset 1 will be examined. The eight most frequent DRGs observed before admission and given in Table 4.31 are compared.

For each DRG, the true positive rate (TP, proportion of cases of that DRG which are correctly classified as belonging to that DRG) and the false positive rate (FP,

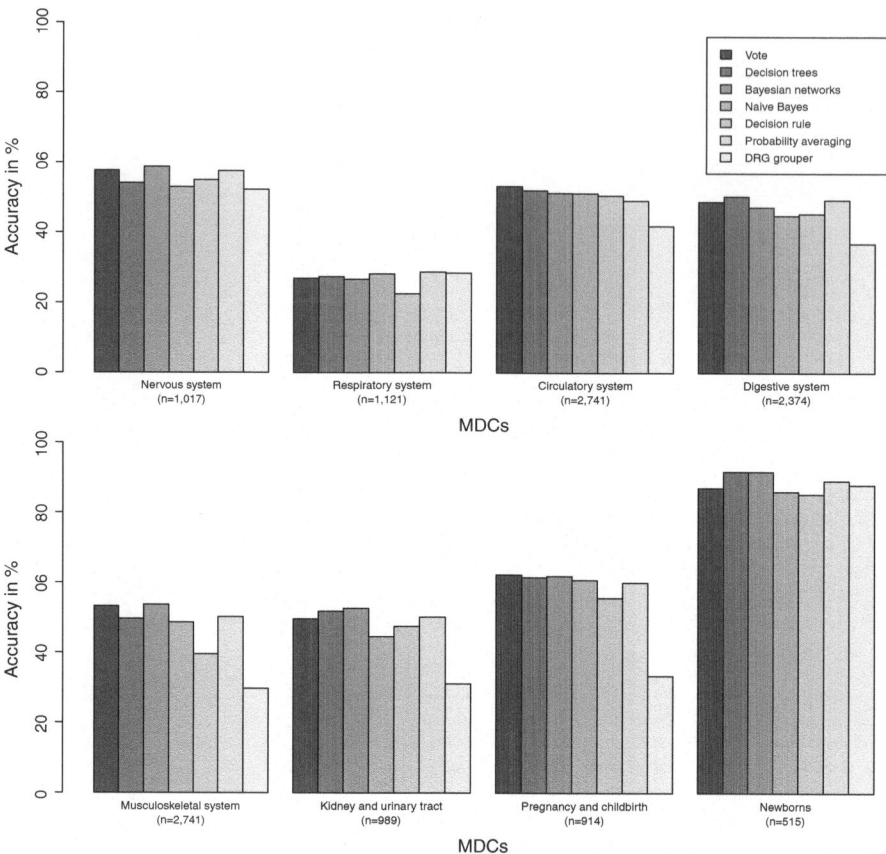

Fig. 4.6 Classification accuracy for different diagnostic categories at admission

proportion of cases of other DRGs which are incorrectly classified as belonging to that DRG) are reported. Table 4.32 shows the class-dependent performance results of the six classification algorithms as compared with the use of the DRG grouper. The table reveals that for DRGs G24Z and I68C the TP rate of the DRG grouper is equal to the TP rate of the machine learning methods. For all other six DRGs, the DRG grouper is outperformed by at least one machine learning approach.

4.1.9.2 Investigation on Selected DRGs at Admission

For the investigation on selected DRGs at admission, dataset 16 is examined. Eight very frequent DRGs given in Table 4.33 are compared, again, with TP and FP as evaluation measures. Table 4.34 shows the class-dependent performance results. In all cases, the TP rates of the machine learning methods are substantially higher

Table 4.31 Selected DRGs and number of cases (*n*) in the dataset before admission

DRG	Description	*n*
F59B	Medium complex cardiovascular incision	80
G24Z	Hernia repair	66
I21Z	Hip replacement	58
I53B	Spine column incision	73
I68C	Non-surgical therapy of the spine column, age > 65 years	183
I68D	Non-surgical therapy of the spine column, age ≤ 65 years	119
L20C	Transurethral incision	65
L64A	Urinary stones and obstruction of the urinary system	80

Table 4.32 TP and FP rates (in %) of the classifiers before admission, broken down by DRG

Algorithm		DRG F59B	G24Z	I21Z	I53B	I68C	I68D	L20C	L64A
NB	TP	**100.0**	95.5	93.1	**100.0**	98.9	97.5	96.9	**100.0**
	FP	0.6	2.5	2.4	0.7	**0.5**	**0.5**	0.9	1.6
BN	TP	96.2	95.5	89.7	97.3	94.5	95.0	96.9	**97.5**
	FP	0.3	0.3	0.3	**0.1**	0.3	0.4	0.2	0.6
Trees	TP	97.5	95.5	89.7	**98.6**	98.9	97.5	90.8	97.5
	FP	0.4	0.1	**0.0**	0.1	3.5	0.4	0.4	0.8
Vote	TP	**100.0**	95.5	89.7	98.6	98.9	96.6	96.9	98.8
	FP	0.5	0.5	0.8	**0.2**	1.0	0.3	0.3	0.9
Rules	TP	96.2	95.5	89.7	95.9	**98.9**	95.8	90.8	88.8
	FP	1.5	0.1	**0.0**	0.1	0.3	0.4	0.3	1.0
PA	TP	97.5	95.5	89.7	98.6	**98.9**	96.6	89.2	95.0
	FP	0.4	**0.1**	**0.1**	**0.1**	0.4	0.3	**0.1**	0.5
Grouper	TP	96.3	95.5	89.7	95.9	**98.9**	95.8	89.2	78.8
	FP	0.3	**0.0**	**0.0**	0.1	0.3	0.2	0.1	0.1

than the ones of the DRG grouper, but FP rates are also typically higher for the machine learning methods. For three of the eight DRGs (B04D, F39B and I44B), each machine learning method is able to correctly classify over 75 % of the cases of the given category, while the DRG grouper does not correctly classify any of these cases. One explanation for this is that in the case of B04D ("extra-cranial surgery", see Table 4.33) the DRG grouper requires the procedure code that leads to DRG B04D. Otherwise, as observed in most of the cases, the alternative DRG B69E ("transient ischemic attack or extra-cranial occlusion") is selected by the DRG grouper. In practice, detailed procedure code documentation takes place after the patients' procedure (e.g. after a surgery) and therefore after the allocation of scarce resources.

Table 4.33 Selected DRGs
and number of cases (*n*)
in the dataset at admission

DRG	Description	*n*
B04D	Extra-cranial surgery	43
B77Z	Headache	87
B80Z	Head injury	267
F39B	Vein stripping	80
F62C	Heart failure	245
F73Z	Collapse or heart disease	321
G67D	Esophagitis	688
I44B	Prosthetic enhancement of the knee	44

Table 4.34 TP and FP rates (in %) of the classifiers at admission, broken down by DRG

		DRG							
Algorithm		B04D	B77Z	B80Z	F39B	F62C	F73Z	G67D	I44B
NB	TP	83.7	81.6	89.8	**96.2**	74.6	84.8	76.2	88.6
	FP	**0.1**	0.3	0.5	**0.1**	3.7	0.8	5.0	0.3
BN	TP	83.7	80.5	87.8	**97.5**	35.8	83.8	61.0	88.6
	FP	**0.1**	0.3	0.2	**0.1**	0.9	0.7	1.9	0.2
Trees	TP	83.7	79.3	85.0	**97.5**	65.4	84.4	76.9	81.8
	FP	**0.1**	0.3	0.2	**0.1**	2.1	0.8	4.2	0.2
Vote	TP	83.7	81.6	87.0	**96.2**	73.8	84.4	72.1	88.6
	FP	**0.1**	0.3	0.2	**0.1**	3.5	0.7	4.2	0.3
Rules	TP	83.7	80.5	86.6	**95.0**	67.1	83.8	75.2	88.6
	FP	**0.1**	0.3	0.2	**0.1**	3.4	0.8	4.6	0.2
PA	TP	83.7	81.6	85.0	**97.5**	40.8	84.4	64.7	77.3
	FP	**0.1**	0.3	0.2	**0.1**	0.8	0.7	2.4	**0.1**
Grouper	TP	0.0	51.8	61.9	0.0	51.4	**63.4**	45.7	0.0
	FP	**0.0**	0.1	0.1	**0.0**	0.3	0.4	0.9	**0.0**

4.1.10   Evaluation of Expected Revenue Estimates

A new measure of misclassification costs that is developed in this dissertation are
error rates of the classifiers with respect to prediction of the expected revenue
for each inpatient. In order to evaluate this, the mean absolute difference in base
revenue (assuming the mean length of stay) between the true and predicted DRGs
are calculated. All values are normalized by dividing through the base rate for the
true DRG. For example, if the true DRG-specific base rate is 2,000 USD for a
given case and the (incorrectly) predicted DRG has a base rate of 2,500 USD, this
corresponds to a mean absolute difference of 0.25.

4.1.10.1   Evaluation of Expected Revenue Estimates Before Admission

The results from the evaluation of expected revenue estimates before admission are
given in Table 4.35.

Table 4.35 Mean absolute differences of the expected revenue for each method

Dataset	Rule	NB	BN	Tree	Vote	PA	DRG grouper
1	0.229	0.349	0.234	0.210	0.208	**0.172**	0.185
2	0.237	0.310	0.231	0.207	0.212	**0.181**	0.192
3	0.642	**0.392**	0.421	0.395	0.393	0.834	1.433
4	0.331	0.394	0.330	0.331	0.344	**0.316**	0.320
5	0.356	0.393	0.364	0.352	0.355	**0.321**	0.327
6	0.642	0.520	0.560	**0.506**	0.507	0.930	1.433
7	0.593	0.476	**0.437**	0.456	0.446	0.439	0.608
8	0.593	0.475	0.481	**0.461**	0.464	0.478	0.611
9	0.642	0.572	0.702	0.587	**0.571**	0.961	1.433
10	0.593	0.511	**0.465**	0.475	0.474	0.507	0.783
11	0.593	0.492	0.519	0.497	**0.477**	0.534	0.784
12	0.642	**0.541**	0.633	0.555	**0.541**	1.076	1.433
Avg.	0.508	0.452	0.448	0.419	**0.416**	0.562	0.795

Table 4.36 Mean absolute differences of the expected revenue for each method

Dataset	Rule	NB	BN	Tree	Vote	PA	DRG grouper
13	0.180	0.251	0.223	0.171	0.174	**0.167**	0.178
14	0.276	0.300	0.305	0.269	0.267	**0.260**	0.270
15	0.366	0.336	0.330	0.323	**0.318**	0.327	0.362
16	0.366	0.346	0.343	0.352	**0.338**	0.368	0.435
Avg.	0.297	0.308	0.300	0.279	**0.274**	0.281	0.311

When using the DRG grouper, the difference of the expected revenue is higher than using machine learning methods. Using the probability averaging approach (which always outperforms the DRG grouper for expected revenue estimates) the mean absolute error for revenue estimation can be reduced in the worst case by 1.4 % and in the best case by 71.9 % for datasets 4 and 3, respectively, as compared to the results of the DRG grouper.

4.1.10.2   Evaluation of Expected Revenue Estimates at Admission

The results at admission are given in Table 4.36 which reveals, similar to the results observed before admission, that at admission the average misclassification costs of each machine learning approach are less than the ones of the DRG grouper. The results show that the mean absolute error for revenue estimation can be reduced in the worst case by 1.1 % and in the best case by 28.7 % for datasets 13 and 16, respectively, as compared to the results of the DRG grouper. The results confirm the benefit of using machine learning techniques for two reasons: First, DRG information can be used for admission control. Viewing a hospital as a profit center, the hospital management seeks to admit as many inpatients as possible having a high prospective revenue as predicted through more accurate early DRG classification.

Second, if a patient's revenue function that is necessary for the scheduling problem developed in this dissertation (see Fig. 3.1) cannot be predicted accurately, and the hospital assigns the wrong revenue function to inpatients, suboptimal resource allocation may occur.

After this evaluation of an efficient approach to early DRG classification, some DRGs will be selected in order to evaluate computationally and economically the scheduling models presented in Chap. 3.

4.2 Computational and Economic Analysis of Scheduling the Hospital-Wide Flow of Elective Patients

This section deals with the computational as well as economic evaluation of the scheduling models based on selected DRGs. Firstly, an overview of the data will be given and the generation of instances will be described. Next, a computation time analysis followed by an economic analysis of the static approaches will be presented. Afterwards, the results of the rolling horizon approach will be provided including an analysis of the lengths of stay as well as the time span between admission and surgery.

4.2.1 Data and Instance Generation

The models presented in Chap. 3 were, as for the machine learning approaches, evaluated on data from the county hospital Erding. The hospital data was joined with data from the German institute for the reimbursement in hospitals (InEK, see Schreyögg et al. [195]). The latter contains the information on the DRG attributes such as (i) low and high LOS trim point, (ii) fixed revenue and (iii) per day reduction and addition. Based on a discussion with the hospital's management the 18 DRGs shown in Table 4.37 were selected because at the time a patient contacts the hospital for admission, these DRGs can be classified with sufficient accuracy. One can observe that the classification accuracies are similar but different to the ones provided in Sect. 4.1.7.1 because in the study of scheduling the hospital-wide flow of elective patients, data from a different year is employed. The table provides the number of patients for each DRG (n), the classification accuracy (Acc.), i.e., the probability of assigning the correct DRG at admission, and the surgery lead time. The surgery lead time is the minimum number of days required for medical activities prior to surgery. Examples are laboratory tests which have to be made prior to an incision or the time required for pre-medication to take effect in the patient's metabolism before surgery. The surgery lead time is guaranteed by setting a minimum time lag between the admission activity and the surgery activity. For the year 2008, the 18 selected DRGs represent 11.6 % of all admitted patients. In the following, it is assumed that these DRGs can be classified with high accuracy

Table 4.37 Statistics for the selected DRGs

DRG	Description	n	Acc. (%)	Surgery lead time (days)
B04D	Extracranial surgery	47	96.6	1
C08B	Cataract surgery	61	100	0
D30B	Tonsillectomy	45	100	0
D38Z	Nose surgery	50	89.4	0
F39B	Vein stripping	138	89.8	0
G24Z	Hernia repair	120	98.4	0
H08B	Laparoscopic cholecystectomy	169	100	0
I44B	Knee arthroplasty	62	93.1	1
I53Z	Spinal disc surgery	139	98.3	0
I68C	Spinal disc therapy (age > 55 years)	260	87.1	0
I68D	Spinal disc therapy (age < 56 years)	165	81.6	0
K12Z	Thyroid surgery	28	88.2	0
L06B	Non-complex urinary bladder incision	70	90.4	0
L20C	Complex urinary bladder incision	132	95.2	0
L64A	Bladder stone (age > 75 years)	127	90.8	0
M02Z	Prostate resection	54	100	0
N21Z	Hysterectomy	52	89.7	1
N25Z	Abrasio	51	82.4	0

at the time the patient or the referring physician contacts the hospital. For the PFP-FA, for each patient $p \in \mathcal{P}$ the admission date α_p is set according to the realized admission date as given by the hospital data. In the case of the PFP-VA the admission time window $\mathcal{W}_{\sigma_p}$ is set according to the realized admission week. For example, if a patient was admitted on Wednesday, then for the PFP-FA α_p is set to that specific Wednesday whereas for the PFP-VA it is required that the patient has to be admitted between Monday and Friday of that specific week. Only 3.8 % of the patients required capacity on the ICU and of them 42.8 % left the ICU within 24 h. For the sake of simplicity, the ICU is modeled as a day resource. Pre- and post-clinical treatments are not considered. Resource capacity $R_{k,t}$ is determined by using the entire capacity of resource $k \in \mathcal{R}$ on day $t \in \mathcal{T}$ minus capacity allocated to patients who do not have the selected DRGs. The order of activities $(i, j) \in \mathcal{E}$ is set according to the order of time stamps in the hospital data. For the capacity demand $r_{i,k}$ of clinical activity i on day resources k, average (avg.) values of the observed distributions are employed. As already stated above, this approach is robust because, first, the capacity demand of activities is a fraction of the available capacity per day, and, second, variance reduction effects can be obtained by summing up the capacity demands of activities assigned to the resource on the same day.

The recovery time of each patient is determined by the difference between the time stamps of the discharge activity and its immediately preceding activity in the clinical pathway. For example, for patient 2 in Fig. 3.2b, activity 7 (stent implementation) immediately precedes activity 8 (discharge). Note that a surgery activity is not always the immediate predecessor of the discharge activity, e.g., for DRG I68C in Table 4.37 a pain therapy activity is the immediate predecessor of the discharge activity.

Table 4.38 Sizes of the problem instances

	$|\mathcal{T}|$		$|\mathcal{P}|$	$|\mathcal{A}|$		$|\mathcal{E}|$		$\frac{1}{|\mathcal{A}|}\sum_{i\in\mathcal{A}}|\mathcal{W}_i|$	
Instance	FA	VA		FA	VA	FA	VA	FA	VA
1	53	52	179	453	632	274	453	5.6	5.3
2	45	45	142	356	498	214	356	5.6	5.5
3	46	46	145	335	480	190	335	5.3	5.6
4	47	45	185	449	634	264	449	5.4	5.2
5	53	52	137	350	487	213	350	5.5	5.5
6	51	48	147	377	524	230	377	5.7	5.2
7	47	46	141	347	488	206	347	5.4	5.3
8	49	50	114	286	400	172	286	5.4	5.6
9	44	42	136	340	476	204	340	5.5	5.2
10	45	46	154	379	533	225	379	5.5	5.5
11	44	44	153	363	516	210	363	5.4	5.6
12	33	34	137	320	457	183	320	5.4	5.6
Avg.	46.4	45.8	147.5	362.9	510.4	215.4	362.9	5.5	5.4

Time windows for activities are determined by using longest path calculation (see Neumann et al. [145]). More precisely, in the case of the PFP-FA, the earliest period of the first activity of a patient p is set equal to the admission date α_p. Then, the earliest periods for all other activities of the patient are calculated using longest path methods. In so doing, the minimum surgery lead time between an activity preceding surgery and the surgery activity itself has to be taken into account for some surgeries (see column "Surgery lead time" in Table 4.37). In order to determine the latest periods L_i, the time window variation parameter w is employed fixing $L_{\phi_p} = E_{\phi_p} + w$. Based on this, the latest periods for all other activities of patient p are determined. For the PFP-VA, the earliest period of the admission activity σ_p is set to the Monday of the week in which the patient was admitted. Then, earliest periods are calculated as for the PFP-FA. The latest period of the discharge activity is determined by $L_{\phi_p} = E_{\phi_p} + 4 + w$. The "4" is added in order to allow for a time window variation parameter of $w = 0$ which ensures that the patient is admitted between Monday and Friday. The time window variation parameter w has been varied between 0 and 6 (see Fig. 4.7).

In total, 12 test instances were generated and indexed by 1, 2, ..., 12. Each one represents all elective patients with the DRGs as provided in Table 4.37 and admitted in month 1, 2, ..., 12 of 2008. Table 4.38 provides the number of patients for each month as well as other key figures when the time window parameter w is set to $w = 4$ for the PFP-FA and $w = 1$ for the PFP-VA.

As can be seen in the last two columns, this choice of w results in time windows of comparable size of the two models which are abbreviated as "FA" and "VA" in the table. The available capacity of the hospital resources has been adjusted by those patients which are not considered in the instances. These are non-elective patients and elective patients with DRGs different from the ones given in Table 4.37.

Table 4.39 Resources and capacities

$k \in \mathcal{R}$	Description	$R_{k,t}$
1–9	Biopsy, endoscopy, functional test, punction, ultrasound, CT, arteriography, nuclear medicine, MRI resources	480 min on workdays, 0 otherwise
10	Operating theater	3,600 min on workdays, 0 otherwise
11	Physical therapy	1,900 min on workdays, 0 otherwise
12	ICU	40 beds on workdays, 90 % of the workday capacity otherwise
13	Ear, nose and throat	155 beds on workdays, 90 % of the workday capacity otherwise
14	Internal medicine	115 beds every day, 90 % of the workday capacity otherwise
15	Surgical specialty	95 beds every day, 90 % of the workday capacity otherwise

Table 4.39 provides the daily capacity of the 12 day and 3 overnight resources before subtracting the expected demand of unplanned patients. For example, the daily operating theater capacity of 3,600 min comes from 6 operating rooms, each one opens from 8 a.m. until 6 p.m. on Monday through Friday.

4.2.2 Computation Time Analysis of the Static Approaches

Table 4.40 shows the number of variables and constraints as well as the computation times. All computations were performed on a 2 GHz PC (Intel Core2 Duo T7250) with 4 GB RAM running Windows 7 64 bit operating system. The models were coded in Java in an ILOG Concert environment. The solver used was ILOG CPLEX 12.2 (64 bit).

4.2.3 Economic Analysis of the Static Approaches

Table 4.41 provides the absolute and relative improvement of the contribution margins obtained by the models when compared to the hospital data. The hospital does not have a formal approach for dealing with the patient flow problem. Instead, it employs a heuristic procedure for deciding on the discharge date and thus patients' LOS. The procedure works as follows. First, the medical criteria always have priority over the economic criteria. That is, a patient is not discharged until fully recovered. As soon as a patient has sufficiently recovered, the discharge decision is based on the marginal contribution margin. The patient is kept in the hospital as long as the marginal contribution margin is increasing and is discharged as soon as it is decreasing.

Table 4.40 Number of decision variables, constraints and solutions times

Instance	#Var. FA	#Var. VA	#Constr. FA	#Constr. VA	Computation time (s) FA	Computation time (s) VA
1	2,558	5,031	1,701	2,402	0.1	0.8
2	1,995	4,135	1,387	1,955	0.1	0.3
3	1,778	4,124	1,360	1,940	0.2	0.4
4	2,435	4,951	1,603	2,313	0.2	0.9
5	1,917	4,036	1,495	2,028	0.2	0.5
6	2,165	4,102	1,519	2,062	0.1	0.5
7	1,886	3,913	1,399	1,948	0.1	0.4
8	1,553	3,350	1,307	1,778	0.1	0.3
9	1,877	3,718	1,340	1,854	0.2	0.3
10	2,067	4,451	1,433	2,064	0.1	0.4
11	1,945	4,430	1,386	1,998	0.1	0.6
12	1,742	3,942	1,135	1,698	0.1	0.4
Avg.	1,993.2	4,181.9	1,422.1	2,003.3	0.1	0.5

Table 4.41 Economic improvement for the static approaches

Instance	Improvement (€) PFP-FA	Improvement (€) PFP-VA	Improvement (%) PFP-FA	Improvement (%) PFP-VA
1	7,252.3	16,976.5	2.3	5.3
2	8,563.9	15,507.5	3.0	5.5
3	13,352.1	16,971.6	5.2	6.6
4	10,470.2	16,497.7	3.0	4.7
5	6,296.4	16,748.8	2.5	6.5
6	8,932.3	15,146.8	3.0	5.1
7	7,577.6	17,932.8	3.2	7.5
8	7,000.0	13,779.2	3.1	6.0
9	12,275.7	15,599.7	4.7	6.0
10	10,969.7	15,749.3	3.9	5.6
11	10,530.4	14,194.3	3.8	5.1
12	9,605.1	14,054.0	4.1	6.0
Avg.	9,402.1	15,763.2	3.5	5.8

The average relative economic improvement for solving the test instances to optimality compared to the hospital solution is 3.5 and 5.8 % when employing the fixed admission date model PFP-FA and the flexible admission date model PFP-VA, respectively. This is equivalent to a monthly increase of the contribution margin of € 9,402.1 for the PFP-FA and of € 15,763.2 for the PFP-VA.

4.2.4 Economic Analysis of the Rolling Horizon Approach

Using data of the first half of 2008 to initialize the probability tables of the Bayesian classifier and to forecast available capacity, the rolling horizon approach is executed

Table 4.42 Economic improvement for the static vs. the rolling horizon approaches		Improvement (€)		Improvement (%)	
		PFP-FA	PFP-VA	PFP-FA	PFP-VA
	Static	46,844.2	47,311.7	6.4	6.5
	Rolling horizon	27,441.0	33,427.0	3.9	5.1

for the third quarter of 2008. When calculating the activity time windows for the rolling horizon approach, the procedure was similar to the static approach with the following modifications. First, for both models, the PFP-FA and the PFP-VA, recovery times were calculated with the Bayesian classifier instead of using realized recovery times. Second, for calculating latest time periods, the latest period of the discharge activity L_{ϕ_p} of patient p is set equal to the maximum DRG-dependent recovery time. With this approach, time windows are obtained which are on average larger than in the static case. In order to make the results comparable, the time window variation parameter was adjusted to $w = 6$ for the fixed admission and to $w = 5$ for the variable admission model leading to a negligible difference between the static and the rolling horizon approach of 0.1 and 0.5 days for the PFP-FA and the PFP-VA, respectively (see Table 4.38).

Table 4.42 gives the gain in contribution margin for the PFP-FA and the PFP-VA when implemented in a static vs. a rolling horizon approach for the third quarter of 2008. Note that the improvement for the static approach is larger than the sum of the improvements for the instances 7–9 (July–September) given in Table 4.41. This is due to the larger time windows which were used in the rolling horizon approach. From Table 4.42 one can see that the improvement of both models compared to the hospital solution is reduced for the more realistic rolling horizon approach. This holds true to a larger extent for PFP-FA. Nevertheless, both approaches and in particular PFP-VA still provide significant improvements compared to the hospital solution. The inferior results of the rolling horizon approach are due to incomplete information. More precisely, for the rolling horizon approach a forecast of the recovery times is used rather than deterministic recovery times. Furthermore, the stochastic resource availability for the first period of each planning run is also considered.

Influence of the time window size on the computation time and relative improvement Figure 4.7a, b show the impact of the time window variation parameter w on the computation time and the relative improvement of PFP-FA and PFP-VA. For increasing time window variation parameter values w the computation time and the economic improvement, compared to the hospital solution, are increasing as well. The increase of the computation time can be observed in particular for the PFP-VA, which considers, when compared to the PFP-FA, the same number of patients but larger networks due to more activities and more precedence constraints. The increase in the improvement is particularly strong for the PFP-FA. The impact on the improvement of the PFP-VA is only small because the latter uses, by definition, larger time window sizes due to the admission time window whereas the PFP-FA uses smaller ones. For both approaches, the PFP-

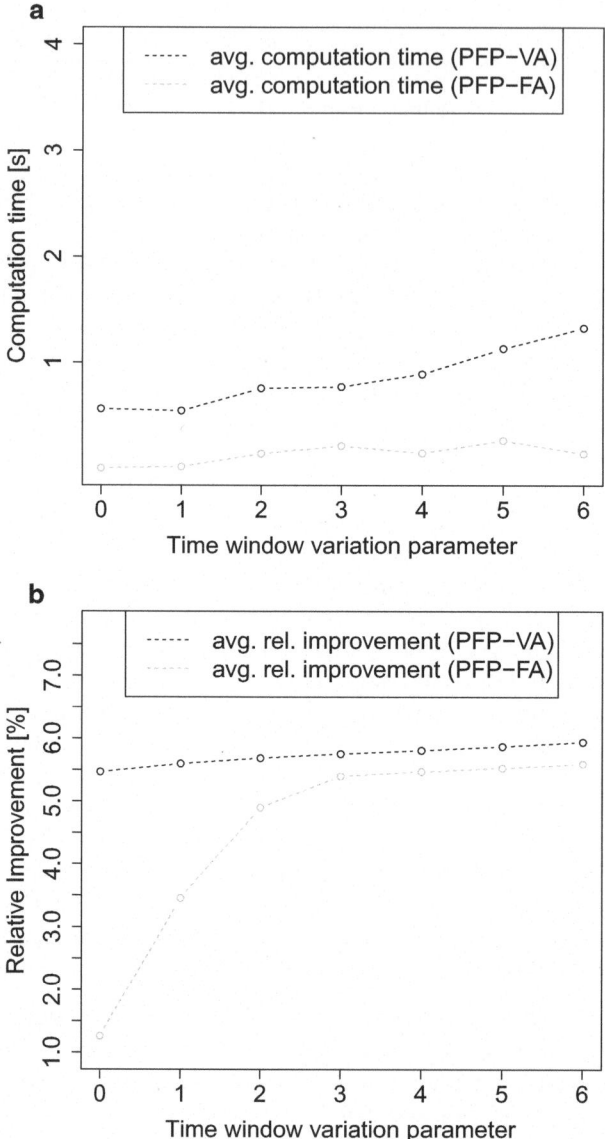

Fig. 4.7 Computation time (**a**) and relative improvement (**b**) as a function of the time window variation parameter w

FA and the PFP-VA, the marginal improvement beyond a time window variation parameter of $w = 3$ is small.

Evaluation of the length of stay and the time admitted patients wait for surgery Figure 4.8a, b provide the frequency distribution for the time span between

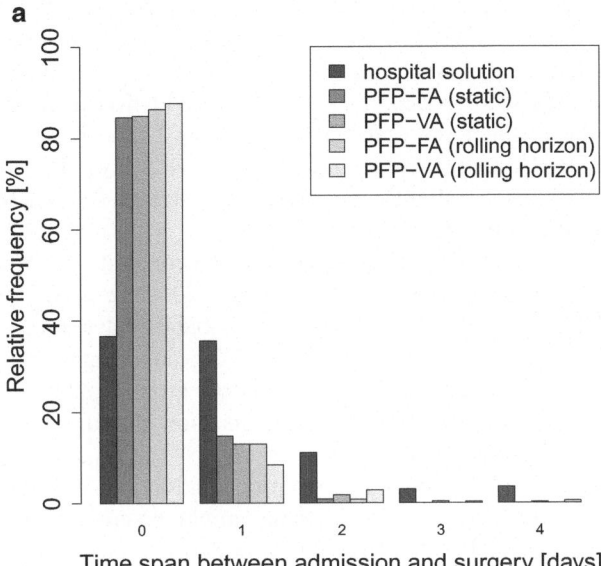

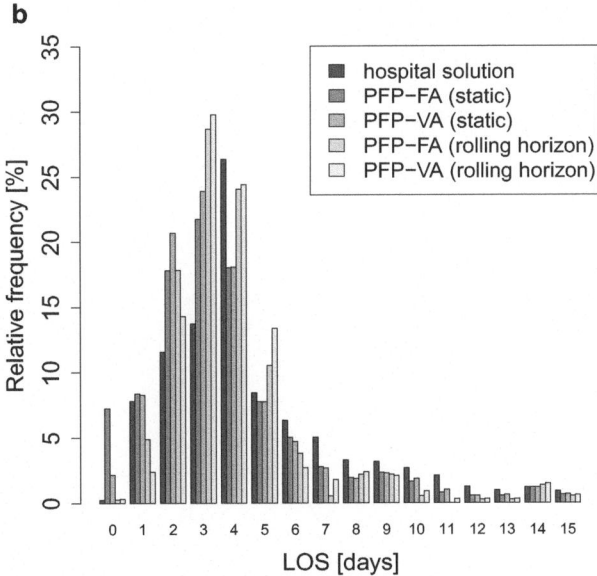

Fig. 4.8 Time span between admission and surgery (**a**) and LOS (**b**)

admission and surgery as well as the length of stay in the hospital. The mathematical models reduce the time span between admission and surgery compared to the hospital solution. In the hospital solution, the difference between the surgery and the admission date is on average 1.8 days. In both, the solutions of the static PFP-FA and the PFP-VA, the average time span between admission and surgery is 0.2 days while it is 0.1 and 0.2 days for the rolling horizon PFP-FA and PFP-VA, respectively. Employing the presented models also leads to a reduction in the length of stay. Compared to the hospital solution with an average LOS of 6.5 days, the static PFP-FA and PFP-VA reduce the length of stay to 4.2 days. The rolling horizon implementation results in a slightly longer length of stay of 4.3 days for the PFP-FA and 4.6 days for the PFP-VA, respectively.

As a result of the experimental analysis, one can conclude that when employing machine learning methods, DRGs can be classified more accurately than when using only a DRG grouper. In particular, the probability averaging approach that combines machine learning methods with the DRG grouper significantly outperform the results as compared to the use of the DRG grouper alone. The results of the hospital-wide scheduling of elective patients show that the scheduling models perform better than the hospital's current approach. The models presented in this work would improve the hospital's economic situation and hospitals of a similar configuration and analogous patient demand might potentially benefit from the approaches developed and evaluated in this dissertation.

Chapter 5
Conclusion

The final chapter summarizes the dissertation and highlights the main research contributions. Areas that deserve further research are also presented.

5.1 Summary

In this dissertation, two problems have been addressed. In Chap. 2, the problem of classifying DRGs of inpatients in early stages of care was presented. Followed by a literature review, a detailed presentation of the two attribute ranking methods information gain and Relief-F was given. Afterwards, three attribute selection methods were presented which are Markov blanket attribute selection, correlation-based feature selection and a wrapper approach. Then, six different classification methods were introduced, namely naive Bayes, Bayesian networks, classification trees, a voting approach, a probability averaging approach and a baseline classifier which is a straightforward decision rule.

Chapter 3 focused on the second problem addressed in this dissertation, namely the problem of scheduling elective patients hospital-wide. After a structured literature review on mathematical programming applied to patient scheduling in hospitals, the problem of scheduling patients hospital-wide with the objective to maximize contribution margin was described. Afterwards, the fixed as well as the variable admission date problems were modeled using mathematical programming. Moreover, a rolling horizon approach was presented in order to evaluate the impact of two sources of uncertainty: Firstly, the hospital-wide resource capacity that is required by emergency patients and the ones for which the DRG cannot be predicted accurately and secondly, uncertain recovery times.

Chapter 4 presented the results of the machine learning experiments as well as the results of solving the scheduling problems. Employing machine learning methods for the early DRG classification has shown that the set of patients' attributes can be reduced to a small set of highly relevant attributes where redundant ones

D. Gartner, *Optimizing Hospital-wide Patient Scheduling*, Lecture Notes in Economics and Mathematical Systems 674, DOI 10.1007/978-3-319-04066-0_5,
© Springer International Publishing Switzerland 2014

can be filtered out. Using subsets of attributes evaluated by attribute ranking and which were chosen by the different attribute selection techniques, the six different classification techniques were compared on the basis of the following four measures: Firstly, the aggregate performance of each classifier was examined, and the learning curves of the different classifiers were evaluated against the use of the DRG grouper. When employed before admission, in connection with attribute selection and assuming that data about admission diagnoses and clinical procedures is available, the combined classification approach achieves up to 79.5 % overall classification accuracy which is significantly larger than using a DRG grouper. Moreover, when used before or at admission and with less assumptions, the proposed probability averaging approach significantly outperforms the DRG grouper. Classification accuracy improves with the number of labeled training examples used for learning, and, even with the worst performing classification approach, data of less than 3,000 patients is necessary to outperform the DRG grouper employed before or at admission. Secondly, on a DRG specific level, the performance of machine learning techniques for the classification of frequently-occurring DRGs was demonstrated. Thirdly, the performance of the classification techniques with respect to classifying patients into MDCs was evaluated. The results demonstrated that at admission, the DRG grouper is outperformed by at least one machine learning approach. Fourthly, the performance of the classification techniques was evaluated with regard to the prediction of expected revenue. Employing this measure, machine learning approaches can reduce the mean absolute error in revenue by up to 71.9 % as compared to the DRG grouper. In conclusion, the proposed classification techniques demonstrate substantial improvements as compared to the existing DRG grouper on each of these measures. Furthermore, significant improvements can be observed when comparing machine learning methods with a straightforward decision rule.

Next, the scheduling problem was studied. In order to evaluate the computational complexity of the task, problem instances were generated based on real-world data and the instances were tested using a commercial solver. After that, the influence of two sources of uncertainty on the economic impact and the patients' length of stay were evaluated. The first source of uncertainty under investigation was uncertain recovery time. The second was uncertain resource capacity as capacity is also required by other patients not included in the study. The time span between surgery and admission, as well as the length of stay, were evaluated employing a rolling horizon approach. The results of solving the scheduling problems have shown that the test instances can be solved in a relatively short computational time. The use of the PFP-FA as well as the PFP-VA can have a significant economic impact on the hospital's contribution margin. The time window size of activities substantially influences the computational time, while the economic improvement can be increased with increasing time window size. A comparison of the hospital solutions and the solutions obtained by employing the mathematical programs reveals that the static PFP-FA shows a relative improvement of 3.5 %, which can even be increased to 5.8 % for variable admission dates. The results of the rolling horizon approach for the PFP-FA show a relative improvement of 3.9 % compared to the contribution margin calculated from the hospital data and 5.1 % for the

PFP-VA. The time span between the admission and the surgery dates can be reduced substantially through both the static and the rolling horizon approach. The results of the rolling horizon approach show a slightly larger time span compared to the static approach. Thus, a strong reduction of LOS was observed for all approaches compared to the hospital data. Moreover, the rolling horizon approach resulted in a longer LOS than the static approaches and yet is shorter than the LOS in the hospital's solution.

5.2 Main Research Contributions

The main research contributions of this dissertation are two-fold. Firstly, the classification of the patient's DRGs using machine learning methods is entirely new. The accuracy evaluation of the approach currently in use, the evaluation of the performance of a straightforward decision rule and the new developed probability averaging approach in comparison with other machine learning methods is among the primary contributions of this dissertation's DRG classification. The promising results of the structured classification accuracy evaluation on different measures and levels can serve as a starting point for future studies (see Sect. 5.3).

The second research contribution is the formulation of the hospital-wide patient scheduling problem. The mathematical models not only consider the highly specific reimbursement structure of hospitals but also take into account the entire patient flow requiring different types of scarce resources. The evaluation of uncertain recovery times, which are continuously updated using a Bayesian prediction of the remaining recovery time, has never been considered before. Therefore, the results of solving and evaluating the scheduling problems addressed in this dissertation can provide yet another starting point for linking Bayesian probabilistic models with scheduling problems.

5.3 Future Research

Having examined the DRG classification at the first contact of elective patients with the hospital and at the admission of all patients, the next logical step is to examine the DRG classification between admission and discharge. As seen in the computational study, the less structured information is available, the more the DRG grouper fails to classify DRGs. However, examining from which point in time after admission the DRG grouper significantly outperforms machine learning methods should be evaluated because the more structured information becomes available the more likely the DRG grouper would benefit from it. Since in this study, longitudinal data about the documentation timestamps of diagnoses was not available, a challenge is first to collect this data from a hospital and then, a longitudinal model for classifying DRGs can be constructed and the convergence of accuracy of the DRG grouper can be compared with the one of the machine learning methods. Another area of future research is to incorporate information of the DRG system specification into the decision tree growing and pruning process. In particular, for rarely occurring DRGs and for the imbalanced DRG distribution, this could be a potential avenue of further research. Finally, an area that deserves additional research is the assessment of the complexity of the classification task performed by humans at each stage of care. Its examination and the evaluation of a trade-off between misclassification costs and the time spent gathering high quality information to improving DRG classification should be undertaken.

Extensions of hospital-wide patient scheduling should take into account additional sources of uncertainty. Those could be potential feedback loops in the clinical pathways where, e.g., laboratory testing results are inconclusive and, thus, tests must be repeated. In project scheduling, this phenomenon commonly arises in the field of research and development. Therefore, it would be useful to evaluate whether methods which were successfully employed in project scheduling fit into the problem structure of hospital-wide patient scheduling. The evaluation of rescheduling decisions is another area requiring further research. The robustness of the schedule (e.g. the robustness of scheduling the admission or the surgery date) should be evaluated in order to avoid patient dissatisfaction. Moreover, the influence of Bayesian recovery time updating on re-scheduling decisions should be undertaken. Finally, the scheduling problem should be extended in order to take into account detailed sequencing decisions within a day and flexible bed allocation decisions for patients that fit to different specialties because of their multi-morbidity.

Appendix A
Notation and List of Abbreviations

Abbreviations

#Constr.	number of constraints
#Var.	number of decision variables
Acc.	classification accuracy
Avg.	average
BN	Bayesian networks
C	continuous
CCL	complication and co-morbidity level
CF	confidence factor
CFS	correlation-based feature selection
contrib.	contribution
CT	computer tomography
DAG	directed acyclic graph
DRGs	diagnosis-related groups
FP	false positive
GB	gigabyte
GHz	gigahertz
GS	grow-shrink algorithm
GSWL	grow-shrink algorithm with whitelisting
IA	incremental-association search
IAWL	incremental-association search with whitelisting
ICD	international statistical classification of diseases and related health problems
ICU	intensive care unit
IG	information gain
InEK	German institute for the reimbursement in hospitals
JCR	journal citation report
LOS	length of stay
MB	Markov blanket
MDC	major diagnostic category

D. Gartner, *Optimizing Hospital-wide Patient Scheduling*, Lecture Notes in Economics and Mathematical Systems 674, DOI 10.1007/978-3-319-04066-0,
© Springer International Publishing Switzerland 2014

MI	minimum number of instances per leaf
Min.	minutes
MIP	mixed-integer programming
MRI	magnetic resonance imaging
N	nominal
NB	naive Bayes
O	ordinal
OR	operating room
OR/MS	operations research and the management sciences
PA	probability averaging
pat.	patient
PC	personal computer
PCCL	patient clinical complexity level
PFP-FA	patient flow problem with fixed admission dates
PFP-VA	patient flow problem with variable admission dates
Pre-MDC	a separate MDC containing DRGs with high-cost procedures
RAM	random access memory
S	string
TP	true positive

Decision Variables

$x_{i,t}$	1, if activity $i \in \mathcal{A}$ is done at day $t \in \mathcal{W}_i$, 0, otherwise
$y_{p,t}$	1, if patient $p \in \mathcal{P}$ has a LOS of $t \in \mathcal{L}_p$ days, 0, otherwise

Sets, Indices and Parameters for the Machine Learning Techniques

$(a \perp\!\!\!\perp b \vert \mathcal{A})$	conditional independence relation between attribute a and attribute $b \neq a$ given attributes $\mathcal{A} \setminus \{a, b\}$
α	significance level
$\mathcal{A}$	set of attributes
$\mathcal{A}_i^*$	optimal attribute subset for the correlation-based feature selection
$\mathcal{D}$	set of DRGs or vertex
$\mathcal{E}$	set of edges
$\mathcal{G} := (\mathcal{V}, \mathcal{E})$	directed acyclic graph
$\mathcal{H}_i(k)$	set of k-nearest hits with respect to instance $i \in \mathcal{I}$
$\mathcal{I}$	set of individuals (hospital inpatients)
$\mathcal{I}_v$	a subset of attribute values $v \in \mathcal{V}_a$ for attribute $a \in \mathcal{A}$
$\mathcal{M}_{d,i}(k)$	set of k-nearest misses with respect to DRG $d \in \mathcal{D}$ and instance $i \in \mathcal{I}$
$\mathcal{S}$	subset of vertices
$\mathcal{V}$	set of vertices
$\mathcal{V}_a$	set of possible values for attribute $a \in \mathcal{A}$

$adj(a)$	set of adjacent vertices of the vertex $a \in \mathcal{V}$
$diff_{i,j,a}$	similarity measure between instances $i, j \in \mathcal{I} : i \neq j$ with respect to attribute $a \in \mathcal{A}$
$diff_{i,j}$	similarity measure between instances $i, j \in \mathcal{I} : i \neq j$
$IG(a)$	information gain of attribute $a \in \mathcal{A}$
$sepSet(a,b) = \mathcal{S}$	a mapping of attributes $\{a,b\}$ to a set $\mathcal{S}$ that separates a from b
$MB(A)$	Markov blanket of attribute A
Π_a	parents of the given attribute $a \in \mathcal{A}$
$A, B, \ldots, F$	attributes or vertices
a, b, c, e, l, g	attributes or vertices
a^*	attribute selected with the highest IG by the decision tree approach
$d_i \in \mathcal{D}$	the true DRG of inpatient $i \in \mathcal{I}$
d_i^*	the DRG assigned to the test instance $i \in \mathcal{I}$
$d_{\max}$	maximum search depth
$H(\mathcal{D}|a)$	conditional information entropy of the set of DRGs $\mathcal{D}$ given an attribute $a \in \mathcal{A}$
$H(\mathcal{D})$	information entropy of the set of DRGs $\mathcal{D}$
$H(d|v)$	conditional information entropy of a DRG $d \in \mathcal{D}$ given an attribute value $v \in \mathcal{V}_a$ of attribute $a \in \mathcal{A}$
k	parameter to define k-nearest hits or misses, respectively
l	iteration of the Relief-F algorithm
n	# attributes in a dataset, # patients in each DRG or MDC
$p(d)$	prior probability for DRG $d \in \mathcal{D}$
$p(v_{i,a}|d)$	conditional probability of attribute value $v_{i,a}$ given DRG d
$p_{c,d}$	probability for DRG d using classifier c
Q_a	quality measure for attribute $a \in \mathcal{A}$
$Q_{a,i}$	quality measure for attribute $a \in \mathcal{A}$ and a sampled instance $i \in \mathcal{I}$
s	number of samples
$U(a,b) \in [0;1]$	symmetrical uncertainty for attribute $a \in \mathcal{A}$ and $b \in \mathcal{A}\backslash a$
$v_{i,a} \in \mathcal{V}_a$	value of attribute $a \in \mathcal{A}$ for inpatient $i \in \mathcal{I}$
$w(a)$	quality measure for attribute $a \in \mathcal{A}$ continuously updated during the Relief-F algorithm

Sets, Indices and Parameters for the Scheduling Problems

$(\mathcal{A}, \mathcal{E})$	graph in which activities $\mathcal{A}$ are represented by nodes and precedence relations $\mathcal{E}$ are represented by arcs
$(i, j) \in \mathcal{E}$	precedence relation for activities $i, j \in \mathcal{A}$
α_p	admission date of patient $p \in \mathcal{P}$
δ	look-ahead parameter for the rolling horizon planning
$\hat{\varrho}_p$	upper bound for the recovery time of patient $p \in \mathcal{P}$

$\mathcal{A}$	set of activities
$\mathcal{A}_p \subset \mathcal{A}$	subset of activities belonging to patient $p \in \mathcal{P}$
$\mathcal{E}$	set of all precedence relations between clinical activities
$\mathcal{L}_p$	set of possible LOSs of patient $p \in \mathcal{P}$
$\mathcal{P}$	set of patients
$\mathcal{R}$	set of all resources
$\mathcal{R}^d$	set of day resources
$\mathcal{R}^n$	set of overnight resources
$\mathcal{T}$	set of periods (days)
$\mathcal{W}_i$	time window of activity $i \in \mathcal{A}$
ϕ_p	discharge activity of patient $p \in \mathcal{P}$
$\pi_{p,t}$	contribution margin for patient $p \in \mathcal{P}$ for lengths of stay $t \in \mathcal{L}_p$
ρ_p	recovery activity for patient $p \in \mathcal{P}$
σ_p	admission activity of patient $p \in \mathcal{P}$
θ	rolling horizon planning iterator
ϖ_p	1, if patient $p \in \mathcal{P}$ has to wait at least 1 day from the admission until the surgery date 0, otherwise
b_p	bed requirement of patient $p \in \mathcal{P}$
$d_{i,j}^{\min} \in \mathbb{Z}_{\geq 0}$	minimum time lag for precedence relation $(i,j) \in \mathcal{E}$
$E[\varrho_p]$	expected recovery time for patient $p \in \mathcal{P}$
$E[R_{k,t}]$	expected capacity of resource $k \in \mathcal{R}$ on day $t \in \mathcal{T}$
E_i	earliest period in which activity $i \in \mathcal{A}$ has to be performed
L_i	latest period in which activity $i \in \mathcal{A}$ has to be performed
n	number of patients within a DRG or MDC
$R_{k,t}^{\text{real}}$	realization of capacity of resource $k \in \mathcal{R}$ at day $t \in \mathcal{T}$
$r_{i,k}$	capacity demand of activity $i \in \mathcal{A}$ from day resource $k \in \mathcal{R}^d$
$R_{k,t}$	capacity of resource $k \in \mathcal{R}$ in period $t \in \mathcal{T}$
S_i^{θ}	vector of start times for activities $i \in \mathcal{A}$ and rolling horizon iteration θ
w	time window variation parameter
z	objective function value

Appendix B
Attributes Assessed and Ranking Results for the Early DRG Classification

Table B.1 provides a detailed overview about all attributes available for the study of early DRG classification. The six admission diagnoses were coded by the referring physician and inserted by the admission nurses into the hospital information system employing ICD codes. Each code contains at least three characters in which the first character is the so-called "medical partition" and the first three characters represent the so-called "category code" (see Bowie and Schaffer [24]). The inpatient's weight is only documented for newborns. The same is true for the attribute "age in days in case of newborns". For each instance, i.e., for each inpatient in each dataset, we generated the additional attributes "DRG calculated by using the DRG grouper", "first three characters of the DRG calculated by using the DRG grouper" and "patient clinical complexity level (PCCL)" calculated at 1st contact and at admission, respectively. PCCL can be determined by taking into account the complication and co-morbidity level (CCL) of each secondary diagnosis with respect to the primary diagnosis (see Schulenburg and Blanke [197]). The motivation for employing PCCL as an additional attribute is because DRG-grouping is sensitive to the clinical complexity of a patient. The more severe secondary diagnoses are documented, with respect to the primary diagnosis, the more likely it is that a "severe DRG" is assigned to a patient.

Table B.1 Attributes assessed for the early DRG classification with continuous (C), nominal (N), ordinal (O) as well as string (S) data types

| | | | Documentation | |
| | | | at 1st contact | at after admission |
Attribute	Data type	Distinct values or bins		
Admission priority	N	3 (non-urgent, admission within next 5 days, admission within next 48 h)	✓	
Age in years documented at 1st contact	C	88 (e.g. 11 years)	✓	
Contact month	N	12 (e.g. December)	✓	
Contact via central bed management	N	2 (yes, no)	✓	
Contact via hotline	N	2 (yes, no)	✓	
Contact via outpatient clinic	N	2 (yes, no)	✓	
Contact weekday	N	7 (e.g. Monday)	✓	
Department documented at 1st contact	N	15 (e.g. department of surgery)	✓	
Diagnosis	S	e.g. "ct", "stent"	✓	
Documentation nurse	N	8 (name of nurse)	✓	
DRG calculated by using the DRG grouper at 1st contact	N	10–341, depending on dataset (e.g. L68B – other moderate illnesses of the urinary tract)	✓	
First three characters of the DRG calculated by using the DRG grouper at 1st contact	N	10–263, depending on dataset (e.g. F72)	✓	
Gender	N	2 (male, female)	✓	
MDC of the DRG calculated by using the DRG grouper at 1st contact	N	27 (e.g. R – symptoms, signs and abnormal clinical and laboratory findings, not elsewhere classified)	✓	
Month of admission documented at 1st contact	N	12 (e.g. December)	✓	
Outpatient	N	2 (yes, no)	✓	
PCCL calculated at 1st contact using the DRG grouper	O	1–5, depending on dataset (no complexity, . . . , severe complexity)	✓	
Referring physician	S	e.g. "Dr. Müller", "Dr.Müller" (with or without blanks)	✓	
Weekday of admission documented at 1st contact	N	7 (e.g. Monday)	✓	
Postal code of the referring physician	N	32 (e.g. 85435)	✓	

(continued)

Table B.1 continued

Attribute	Data type	Distinct values or bins	Documentation at 1st contact	at after admission
Admission diagnosis 1	N	2,251 (e.g. R55 – syncope and collapse, R10.4 – other and unspecified abdominal pain)		✓
Admission diagnosis 2	N	1,668 (e.g. see admission diagnosis 1)		✓
Admission diagnosis 3	N	1,052 (e.g. see admission diagnosis 1)		✓
Admission diagnosis 4	N	700 (e.g. see admission diagnosis 1)		✓
Admission diagnosis 5	N	498 (e.g. see admission diagnosis 1)		✓
Admission diagnosis 6	N	360 (e.g. see admission diagnosis 1)		✓
Age in days in case of newborns	C	8 (0 days, 1 day, 2 days, 3 days, 4 days, 5 days, 8 days, 238 days)		✓
Age in years documented at admission	C	101 (0 years, 1 year, ..., 99 years, 102 years)		✓
Category code of admission diagnosis 1	N	823 (e.g. H60 – otitis externa)		✓
Category code of admission diagnosis 2	N	731 (e.g. see category code of admission diagnosis 1)		✓
Category code of admission diagnosis 3	N	565 (e.g. see category code of admission diagnosis 1)		✓
Category code of admission diagnosis 4	N	415 (e.g. see category code of admission diagnosis 1)		✓
Category code of admission diagnosis 5	N	298 (e.g. see category code of admission diagnosis 1)		✓
Category code of admission diagnosis 6	N	226 (e.g. see category code of admission diagnosis 1)		✓
Days in hospital before admission	C	10 (0 days, ..., 9 days)		✓
Department documented at admission	N	40 (e.g. department of surgery, intensive care unit)		✓
DRG calculated by using the DRG grouper at admission	N	202–503, depending on dataset (e.g. F72B – unstable angina pectoris)		✓
First three characters of the DRG calculated by using the DRG grouper at admission	N	142–363, depending on dataset (e.g. "F72")		✓
Hour of admission	N	24 (e.g. 10 a.m.)		✓

(continued)

Table B.1 continued

Attribute	Data type	Distinct values or bins	Documentation at 1st contact	at after admission
MDC of the DRG calculated by using the DRG grouper at admission	N	27, equal number for all datasets (e.g. R – symptoms, signs and abnormal clinical and laboratory findings, not elsewhere classified)	✓	
Medical partition of admission diagnosis 1	N	21 (e.g. R – symptoms, signs and abnormal clinical and laboratory findings, not elsewhere classified)	✓	
Medical partition of admission diagnosis 2	N	26 (e.g. see medical partition of admission diagnosis 1)	✓	
Medical partition of admission diagnosis 3	N	25 (e.g. see medical partition of admission diagnosis 1)	✓	
Medical partition of admission diagnosis 4	N	23 (e.g. see medical partition of admission diagnosis 1)	✓	
Medical partition of admission diagnosis 5	N	22 (e.g. R – symptoms, signs and abnormal clinical and laboratory findings, not elsewhere classified)	✓	
Medical partition of admission diagnosis 6	N	20 (e.g. see medical partition of admission diagnosis 1)	✓	
Month of admission	N	12 (e.g. December)	✓	
PCCL calculated at admission using a DRG grouper	O	5 (equal number for all datasets) (no complexity, …, severe complexity)	✓	
Reason for admission	N	5 (complete inpatient treatment, inpatient treatment with preliminary outpatient treatment, delivery, childbirth, pre-inpatient treatment)	✓	
Type of admission	N	4 (referral, emergency admission, transferring from another hospital, childbirth)	✓	
Weekday of admission	N	7 (e.g. Monday)	✓	
Weight at admission in case of newborns	C	290 (e.g. 2,100 g)	✓	
Procedure section of procedure codes	N	0–6, depending on data set (e.g. 5 – surgeries)		✓
First three-digits of procedure codes	N	0–169, depending on data set (e.g. 542 – esophagus surgeries)		✓
Procedure codes	N	0–2,468, depending on data set (e.g. 5423 – partial esophagus resection)		✓
DRG (class attribute)	N	635 (e.g. F72B – Unstable angina pectoris)	Calculated at discharge	

Table B.2 Results of the top three attributes of the IG attribute ranking for each dataset before admission

Data-set	Rank 1	IG	Rank 2	IG	Rank 3	IG
1	DRG calculated by using the DRG grouper at 1st contact	6.555	First three characters of the DRG calculated by using the DRG grouper at 1st contact	6.264	Admission diagnosis 1	5.929
2	DRG calculated by using the DRG grouper at 1st contact	6.532	First three characters of the DRG calculated by using the DRG grouper at 1st contact	6.246	Admission diagnosis 1	5.929
3	Department documented at 1st contact	3.027	Postal code of the referring physician	0.873	Contact month	0.778
4	DRG calculated by using the DRG grouper at 1st contact	6.266	First three characters of the DRG calculated by using the DRG grouper at 1st contact	5.981	Admission diagnosis 1	5.929
5	DRG calculated by using the DRG grouper at 1st contact	6.238	First three characters of the DRG calculated by using the DRG grouper at 1st contact	5.962	Admission diagnosis 1	5.929
6	Department documented at 1st contact	3.027	Postal code of the referring physician	0.873	Contact month	0.778
7	Admission diagnosis 1	5.929	DRG calculated by using the DRG grouper at 1st contact	5.616	Category code of admission diagnosis 1	5.444
8	Admission diagnosis 1	5.929	DRG calculated by using the DRG grouper at 1st contact	5.593	Category code of admission diagnosis 1	5.444
9	Department documented at 1st contact	3.027	Postal code of the referring physician	0.873	Contact month	0.778
10	Admission diagnosis 1	5.929	Category code of admission diagnosis 1	5.444	DRG calculated by using the DRG grouper at 1st contact	4.607
11	Admission diagnosis 1	5.929	Category code of admission diagnosis 1	5.444	DRG calculated by using the DRG grouper at 1st contact	4.585
12	Department documented at 1st contact	3.027	Postal code of the referring physician	0.873	Contact month	0.778

Table B.3 Results of the top three attributes of the IG attribute ranking for each dataset at admission

Data-set	Rank 1	IG	Rank 2	G	Rank 3	IG
13	DRG calculated by using the DRG grouper at admission	5.85	Admission diagnosis 1	5.65	First three characters of the DRG calculated by using the DRG grouper at admission	5.642
14	Admission diagnosis 1	5.65	DRG calculated by using the DRG grouper at admission	5.493	First three characters of the DRG calculated by using the DRG grouper at admission	5.3
15	Admission diagnosis 1	5.65	Category code of admission diagnosis 1	5.182	DRG calculated by using the DRG grouper at admission	5.151
16	Admission diagnosis 1	5.65	Category code of admission diagnosis 1	5.182	DRG calculated by using the DRG grouper at admission	4.61

Table B.4 Results of the top three attributes of the Relief-F attribute ranking for each dataset before admission

Data-set	Rank 1	Q_a	Rank 2	Q_a	Rank 3	Q_a
1	First three characters of the DRG calculated by using the DRG grouper at 1st contact	0.804	DRG calculated by using the DRG grouper at 1st contact	0.793	Department documented at 1st contact	0.754
2	First three characters of the DRG calculated by using the DRG grouper at 1st contact	0.806	DRG calculated by using the DRG grouper at 1st contact	0.795	Department documented at 1st contact	0.756
3	Department documented at 1st contact	0.755	5	0.383	8	0.309
4	Department documented at 1st contact	0.755	First three characters of the DRG calculated by using the DRG grouper at 1st contact	0.731	DRG calculated by using the DRG grouper at 1st contact	0.721
5	Department documented at 1st contact	0.756	First three characters of the DRG calculated by using the DRG grouper at 1st contact	0.735	DRG calculated by using the DRG grouper at 1st contact	0.725
6	Department documented at 1st contact	0.755	5	0.374	Contact via hotline	0.243

(continued)

Table B.4 continued

Data-set	Rank 1	Q_a	Rank 2	Q_a	Rank 3	Q_a
7	Department documented at 1st contact	0.755	MDC of the DRG calculated by using the DRG grouper at 1st contact	0.715	First three characters of the DRG calculated by using the DRG grouper at 1st contact	0.676
8	Department documented at 1st contact	0.756	MDC of the DRG calculated by using the DRG grouper at 1st contact	0.714	First three characters of the DRG calculated by using the DRG grouper at 1st contact	0.679
9	Department documented at 1st contact	0.756	5	0.308	Contact via hotline	0.246
10	Department documented at 1st contact	0.754	MDC of the DRG calculated by using the DRG grouper at 1st contact	0.715	First three characters of the DRG calculated by using the DRG grouper at 1st contact	0.685
11	Department documented at 1st contact	0.756	MDC of the DRG calculated by using the DRG grouper at 1st contact	0.715	First three characters of the DRG calculated by using the DRG grouper at 1st contact	0.69
12	Department documented at 1st contact	0.757	Contact via hotline	0.24	Postal code of the referring physician	0.212

Table B.5 Results of the top three attributes of the Relief-F attribute ranking for each dataset at admission

Data-set	Rank 1	Q_a	Rank 2	Q_a	Rank 3	Q_a
13	First three characters of the DRG calculated by using the DRG grouper at admission	0.735	MDC of the DRG calculated by using the DRG grouper at admission	0.722	DRG calculated by using the DRG grouper at admission	0.718
14	MDC of the DRG calculated by using the DRG grouper at admission	0.716	First three characters of the DRG calculated by using the DRG grouper at admission	0.691	DRG calculated by using the DRG grouper at admission	0.675
15	MDC of the DRG calculated by using the DRG grouper at admission	0.714	First three characters of the DRG calculated by using the DRG grouper at admission	0.676	DRG calculated by using the DRG grouper at admission	0.658
16	MDC of the DRG calculated by using the DRG grouper at admission	0.717	First three characters of the DRG calculated by using the DRG grouper at admission	0.69	DRG calculated by using the DRG grouper at admission	0.67

Bibliography

1. http://www.scopus.com. Last accessed 22 May 2013
2. ISI Web of Knowledge Journal Citation Report (JCR) 2011, Thomson Reuters, http://webofknowledge.com. Last accessed 22 May 2013
3. *Weiterentwicklung des G-DRG-Systems für das Jahr 2008: Klassifikation, Katalog und Bewertungsrelationen.* InEK – Institut für das Entgeltsystem im Krankenhaus, Siegburg, 2007
4. M. Abad-Grau, J. Ierache, C. Cervino, P. Sebastiani, Evolution and challenges in the design of computational systems for triage assistance. J. Biomed. Inform. **41**(3), 432–441 (2008)
5. R. Acharya, O. Faust, A. Alvin, S. Sree, F. Molinari, L. Saba, A. Nicolaides, J. Suri, Symptomatic vs. asymptomatic plaque classification in carotid ultrasound. J. Med. Syst. **36**(3), 1861–1871 (2012)
6. M. Aldape-Pérez, C. Yáñez Márquez, O. Camacho-Nieto, A.J. Argüelles-Cruz, An associative memory approach to medical decision support systems. Comput. Methods Programs Biomed. **106**(3), 287–307 (2012)
7. F. Alemi, M. Torii, M. Atherton, D. Pattie, K. Cox, Bayesian processing of context-dependent text: reasons for appointments can improve detection of influenza. Med. Decis. Mak. **32**(2), 1–9 (2012)
8. C.F. Aliferis, A. Statnikov, I. Tsamardinos, S. Mani, X.D. Koutsoukos, Local causal and Markov blanket induction for causal discovery and feature selection for classification Part I: algorithms and empirical evaluation. J. Mach. Learn. Res. **11**(1), 171–234 (2010)
9. K. Ambert, A. Cohen, A system for classifying disease comorbidity status from medical discharge summaries using automated hotspot and negated concept detection. J. Am. Med. Inform. Assoc. **16**(4), 590–595 (2009)
10. R. Anthony, *Planning and Control Systems: A Framework for Analysis* (Harvard Business School Division of Research Press, Boston, 1965)
11. C. Arizmendi, A. Vellido, E. Romero, Classification of human brain tumours from MRS data using discrete wavelet transform and Bayesian neural networks. Expert Syst. Appl. **39**(5), 5223–5232 (2012)
12. L. Atallah, B. Lo, R. Ali, R. King, G.-Z. Yang, Real-time activity classification using ambient and wearable sensors. IEEE Trans. Inf. Technol. Biomed. **13**(6), 1031–1039 (2009)
13. V. Augusto, X. Xie, V. Perdomo, Operating theatre scheduling with patient recovery in both operating rooms and recovery beds. Comput. Ind. Eng. **58**(2), 231–238 (2010)
14. O. Aziz, L. Atallah, B. Lo, E. Gray, T. Athanasiou, A. Darzi, G.-Z. Yang, Ear-worn body sensor network device: an objective tool for functional postoperative home recovery monitoring. J. Am. Med. Inform. Assoc. **18**(2), 156–159 (2011)
15. M. Bacauskiene, A. Verikas, A. Gelzinis, A. Vegiene, Random forests based monitoring of human larynx using questionnaire data. Expert Syst. Appl. **39**(5), 5506–5512 (2012)

16. X. Bai, R. Padman, J. Ramsey, P. Spirtes, Tabu search-enhanced graphical models for classification in high dimensions. INFORMS J. Comput. **20**(3), 423–437 (2008)
17. M. Banerjee, Y. Ding, A.-M. Noone, Identifying representative trees from ensembles. Stat. Med. **31**(15), 1601–1616 (2012)
18. J. Bard, Y. Shao, H. Wang, Weekly scheduling models for traveling therapists. Socio-Econ. Plan. Sci. **47**(3), (2013)
19. V. Baskaran, A. Guergachi, R. Bali, R. Naguib, Predicting breast screening attendance using machine learning techniques. IEEE Trans. Inf. Technol. Biomed. **15**(2), 251–259 (2011)
20. S. Batun, B. Denton, T. Huschka, A. Schaeffer, Operating room pooling and parallel surgery processing under uncertainty. INFORMS J. Comput. **23**(2), 220–237 (2011)
21. D. Bertsimas, M. Bjarnadóttir, M. Kane, J. Kryder, R. Pandey, S. Vempala, G. Wang, Algorithmic prediction of health-care costs. Oper. Res. **56**(6), 1382–1392 (2008)
22. C. Bishop, *Pattern Recognition and Machine Learning* (Springer, New York, 2006)
23. C.K. Botz, Principles for funding on a case mix basis: construction of case weights (RIWs). Healthc. Manag. Forum **4**(4), 22–32 (1991)
24. M. Bowie, R. Schaffer, *Understanding ICD-10-CM and ICD-10-PCS Coding: A Worktext.* (Cengage Learning, Clifton Park, 2010)
25. A. Boxwala, J. Kim, J. Grillo, L. Ohno-Machado, Using statistical and machine learning to help institutions detect suspicious access to electronic health records. J. Am. Med. Inform. Assoc. **18**(4), 498–505 (2011)
26. N. Boysen, M. Fliedner, A. Scholl, A classification of assembly line balancing problems. Eur. J. Oper. Res. **183**(2), 674–693 (2007)
27. M.L. Brandeau, F. Sainfort, W.P. Pierskalla (eds.), *Operations Research and Health Care.* Volume 70 of Kluwer International Series in Operations Research & Management Science (Springer, New York, 2004)
28. M. Budnik, B. Krawczyk, On optimal settings of classification tree ensembles for medical decision support. Health Inform. J. **19**(1), 3–15 (2013)
29. R. Busse, A. Geissler, W. Quentin, M. Wiley, *Diagnosis-Related Groups in Europe* (McGraw-Hill, Berkshire, 2011)
30. R. Busse, U. Nimptsch, T. Mansky, Measuring, monitoring and managing quality in Germany's hospitals. Health Aff. **28**(2), 294–304 (2009)
31. B. Cardoen, E. Demeulemeester, A decision support system for surgery sequencing at UZ Leuven's day-care department. Int. J. Inf. Technol. Decis. Mak. **10**(3), 435–450 (2011)
32. B. Cardoen, E. Demeulemeester, J. Beliën, Optimizing a multiple objective surgical case sequencing problem. Int. J. Prod. Econ. **119**(2), 354–366 (2009)
33. B. Cardoen, E. Demeulemeester, J. Beliën, Sequencing surgical cases in a day-care environment: an exact branch-and-price approach. Comput. Oper. Res. **36**(9), 2660–2669 (2009)
34. B. Cardoen, E. Demeulemeester, J. Beliën, Operating room planning and scheduling: a literature review. Eur. J. Oper. Res. **201**(3), 921–932 (2010)
35. S. Ceschia, A. Schaerf, Local search and lower bounds for the patient admission scheduling problem. Comput. Oper. Res. **38**(10), 1452–1463 (2011)
36. S. Chaabane, N. Meskens, A. Guinet, M. Laurent, Comparison of two methods of operating theatre planning: application in Belgian hospital. J. Syst. Sci. Syst. Eng. **17**(2), 171–186 (2008)
37. C.-L. Chang, C.-H. Chen, Applying decision tree and neural network to increase quality of dermatologic diagnosis. Expert Syst. Appl. **36**(2), 4035–4041 (2009)
38. P.-C. Chang, J.-J. Lin, C.-H. Liu, An attribute weight assignment and particle swarm optimization algorithm for medical database classifications. Comput. Methods Programs Biomed. **107**(3), 382–392 (2012)
39. G. Chen, J. Warren, P. Riddle, Semantic space models for classification of consumer webpages on metadata attributes. J. Biomed. Inform. **43**(5), 725–735 (2010)

40. B. Cho, H. Yu, K.-W. Kim, T. Kim, I. Kim, S. Kim, Application of irregular and unbalanced data to predict diabetic nephropathy using visualization and feature selection methods. Artif. Intell. Med. **42**(1), 37–53 (2008)

41. B. Cho, H. Yu, J. Lee, Y. Chee, I. Kim, S. Kim, Nonlinear support vector machine visualization for risk factor analysis using nomograms and localized radial basis function kernels. IEEE Trans. Inf. Technol. Biomed. **12**(2), 247–256 (2008)

42. V. Chow, M. Puterman, N. Salehirad, W. Huang, D. Atkins, Reducing surgical ward congestion through improved surgical scheduling and uncapacitated simulation. Prod. Oper. Manag. **20**(3), 418–430 (2011)

43. A. Chu, H. Ahn, B. Halwan, B. Kalmin, E. Artifon, A. Barkun, M. Lagoudakis, A. Kumar, A decision support system to facilitate management of patients with acute gastrointestinal bleeding. Artif. Intell. Med. **42**(3), 247–259 (2008)

44. D. Conforti, F. Guerriero, R. Guido, Optimization models for radiotherapy patient scheduling. 4OR: Q. J. Oper. Res. **6**(3), 263–278 (2008)

45. D. Conforti, F. Guerriero, R. Guido, Non-block scheduling with priority for radiotherapy treatments. Eur. J. Oper. Res. **201**(1), 289–296 (2010)

46. D. Conforti, F. Guerriero, R. Guido, M. Cerinic, M. Conforti, An optimal decision making model for supporting week hospital management. Health Care Manag. Sci. **14**(1), 74–88 (2011)

47. M. Conway, S. Doan, A. Kawazoe, N. Collier, Classifying disease outbreak reports using n-grams and semantic features. Int. J. Med. Inform. **78**(12), 47–58 (2009)

48. A. Daemen, D. Timmerman, T. Van den Bosch, C. Bottomley, E. Kirk, C. Van Holsbeke, L. Valentin, T. Bourne, B. De Moor, Improved modeling of clinical data with kernel methods. Artif. Intell. Med. **54**(2), 103–114 (2012)

49. D. Delen, C. Fuller, C. McCann, D. Ray, Analysis of healthcare coverage: a data mining approach. Expert Syst. Appl. **36**(2), 995–1003 (2009)

50. D. Delen, A. Oztekin, L. Tomak, An analytic approach to better understanding and management of coronary surgeries. Decis. Support Syst. **52**(3), 698–705 (2012)

51. P. Demeester, W. Souffriau, P. De Causmaecker, G. Vanden Berghe, A hybrid tabu search algorithm for automatically assigning patients to beds. Artif. Intell. Med. **48**(1), 61–70 (2009)

52. J. Denny, A. Spickard, K. Johnson, N. Peterson, J. Peterson, R. Miller, Evaluation of a method to identify and categorize section headers in clinical documents. J. Am. Med. Inform. Assoc. **16**(6), 806–815 (2009)

53. B. Denton, D. Gupta, A sequential bounding approach for optimal appointment scheduling. IIE Trans. **35**(11), 1003–1016 (2003)

54. B. Denton, A. Miller, H. Balasubramanian, T. Huschka, Optimal allocation of surgery blocks to operating rooms under uncertainty. Oper. Res. **58**(4), 802–816 (2010)

55. B. Denton, J. Viapiano, A. Vogl, Optimization of surgery sequencing and scheduling decisions under uncertainty. Health Care Manag. Sci. **10**(1), 13–24 (2007)

56. J. DeShazo, A. Turner, An interactive and user-centered computer system to predict physician's disease judgments in discharge summaries. J. Biomed. Inform. **43**(2), 218–223 (2010)

57. S. Dreiseitl, L. Ohno-Machado, Logistic regression and artificial neural network classification models: a methodology review. J. Biomed. Inform. **35**(5–6), 352–359 (2002)

58. R. Erol, S. Oğulata, C. Şahin, Z. Alparslan, A radial basis function neural network (RBFNN) approach for structural classification of thyroid diseases. J. Med. Syst. **32**(3), 215–220 (2008)

59. L. Fan, K.-L. Poh, P. Zhou, Partition-conditional ICA for Bayesian classification of microarray data. Expert Syst. Appl. **37**(12), 8188–8192 (2010)

60. Y.-J. Fan, W. Chaovalitwongse, Optimizing feature selection to improve medical diagnosis. Ann. Oper. Res. **174**(1), 169–183 (2010)

61. R. Farkas, G. Szarvas, I. Hegedüs, A. Almási, V. Vincze, R. Ormándi, R. Busa-Fekete, Semi-automated construction of decision rules to predict morbidities from clinical texts. J. Am. Med. Inform. Assoc. **16**(4), 601–605 (2009)

62. H. Fei, C. Chu, N. Meskens, Solving a tactical operating room planning problem by a column-generation-based heuristic procedure with four criteria. Ann. Oper. Res. **166**(1), 91–108 (2009)
63. H. Fei, C. Chu, N. Meskens, A. Artiba, Solving surgical cases assignment problem by a branch-and-price approach. Int. J. Prod. Econ. **112**(1), 96–108 (2008)
64. H. Fei, N. Meskens, C. Chu, A planning and scheduling problem for an operating theatre using an open scheduling strategy. Comput. Ind. Eng. **58**(2), 221–230 (2010)
65. H. Fei, N. Meskens, C. Combes, C. Chu, The endoscopy scheduling problem: a case study with two specialised operating rooms. Int. J. Prod. Econ. **120**(2), 452–462 (2009)
66. G. Fiol, P. Haug, Classification models for the prediction of clinicians' information needs. J. Biomed. Inform. **42**(1), 82–89 (2009)
67. C. Frantzidis, C. Bratsas, M. Klados, E. Konstantinidis, C. Lithari, A. Vivas, C. Papadelis, E. Kaldoudi, C. Pappas, P. Bamidis, On the classification of emotional biosignals evoked while viewing affective pictures: an integrated data-mining-based approach for healthcare applications. IEEE Trans. Inf. Technol. Biomed. **14**(2), 309–318 (2010)
68. O. Frunza, D. Inkpen, S. Matwin, W. Klement, P. O'Blenis, Exploiting the systematic review protocol for classification of medical abstracts. Artif. Intell. Med. **51**(1), 17–25 (2011)
69. S. Fu, M. Desmarais, Tradeoff analysis of different Markov blanket local learning approaches, in *Advances in Knowledge Discovery and Data Mining*, ed. by T. Washio, E. Suzuki, K. Ting, A. Inokuchi. Volume 5012 of Lecture Notes in Computer Science (Springer, Berlin/Heidelberg, 2008), pp. 562–571
70. D. Gartner, R. Kolisch, Scheduling the hospital-wide flow of elective patients. Eur. J. Oper. Res. **233**(3), (2014)
71. S. Ghazavi, T. Liao, Medical data mining by fuzzy modeling with selected features. Artif. Intell. Med. **43**(3), 195–206 (2008)
72. M. Gietzelt, G. Nemitz, K.-H. Wolf, H. Meyer zu Schwabedissen, R. Haux, M. Marschollek, A clinical study to assess fall risk using a single waist accelerometer. Inform. Health Soc. Care **34**(4), 181–188 (2009)
73. D. Glotsos, I. Kalatzis, P. Theocharakis, P. Georgiadis, A. Daskalakis, K. Ninos, P. Zoumboulis, A. Filippidou, D. Cavouras, A multi-classifier system for the characterization of normal, infectious, and cancerous prostate tissues employing transrectal ultrasound images. Comput. Methods Programs Biomed. **97**(1), 53–61 (2010)
74. I. Goldstein, O. Uzuner, Specializing for predicting obesity and its co-morbidities. J. Biomed. Inform. **42**(5), 873–886 (2009)
75. J. Goodson, W. Jang, Assessing nursing home care quality through Bayesian networks. Health Care Manag. Sci. **11**(4), 382–392 (2008)
76. J. Griffiths, J. Williams, R. Wood, Scheduling physiotherapy treatment in an inpatient setting. Oper. Res. Health Care **1**(4), 65–72 (2012)
77. T. Grubinger, C. Kobel, K.-P. Pfeiffer, Regression tree construction by bootstrap: model search for DRG-systems applied to Austrian health-data. BMC Med. Inform. Decis. Mak. **10**(9), 1–11 (2010)
78. F. Guerriero, R. Guido, Operational research in the management of the operating theatre: a survey. Health Care Manag. Sci. **14**(1), 89–114 (2011)
79. A. Guinet, S. Chaabane, Operating theatre planning. Int. J. Prod. Econ. **85**(1), 69–81 (2003)
80. M. Hall, G. Holmes, Benchmarking attribute selection techniques for discrete class data mining. IEEE Trans. Knowl. Data Eng. **15**(6), 1437–1447 (2003)
81. R. Hall (ed.), *Patient Flow: Reducing Delay in Healthcare Delivery*. Volume 91 of Springer International Series in Operations Research & Management Science (Springer, New York, 2006)
82. R. Hall (ed.), *Handbook of Health Care Systems Scheduling*. Volume 168 of Springer International Series in Operations Research & Management Science (Springer, New York, 2011)
83. T. Hanne, T. Melo, S. Nickel, Bringing robustness to patient flow management through optimized patient transports in hospitals. Interfaces **39**(3), 241–255 (2009)

84. E.W. Hans, M. van Houdenhoven, P.J.H. Hulshof, A framework for health care planning and control, in *Handbook of Health Care Systems Scheduling*, ed. by R. Hall. Volume 168 of Springer International Series in Operations Research & Management Science, chapter 12 (Springer, New York, 2011), pp. 303–320

85. M. Hariharan, L. Chee, S. Yaacob, Analysis of infant cry through weighted linear prediction cepstral coefficients and probabilistic neural network. J. Med. Syst. **36**(3), 1309–1315 (2012)

86. P. Harper, A review and comparison of classification algorithms for medical decision making. Health Policy **71**(3), 315–331 (2005)

87. R.C. Holte, Very simple classification rules perform well on most commonly used datasets. Mach. Learn. **11**(1), 63–90 (1993)

88. N.-C. Hsieh, L.-P. Hung, C.-C. Shih, H.-C. Keh, C.-H. Chan, Intelligent postoperative morbidity prediction of heart disease using artificial intelligence techniques. J. Med. Syst. **36**(3), 1809–1820 (2012)

89. Y. Hu, T. Ku, R. Jan, K. Wang, Y. Tseng, S. Yang, Decision tree-based learning to predict patient controlled analgesia consumption and readjustment. BMC Med. Inform. Decis. Mak. **12**(11), 131 (2012)

90. Y.-H. Hu, F. Wu, C.-L. Lo, C.-T. Tai, Predicting warfarin dosage from clinical data: a supervised learning approach. Artif. Intell. Med. **56**(1), 27–34 (2012)

91. S. Huang, L. Wulsin, H. Li, J. Guo, Dimensionality reduction for knowledge discovery in medical claims database: application to antidepressant medication utilization study. Comput. Methods Programs Biomed. **93**(2), 115–123 (2009)

92. P.J. Hulshof, N. Kortbeek, R.J. Boucherie, E.W. Hans, Taxonomic classification of planning decisions in health care: a review of the state of the art in OR/MS. Health Syst. **1**(2), 129–175 (2012)

93. K. Iserson, J. Moskop, Triage in medicine, Part I: concept, history, and types. Ann. Emerg. Med. **49**(3), 275–281 (2007)

94. N. Ishii, A. Koike, Y. Yamamoto, T. Takagi, Figure classification in biomedical literature to elucidate disease mechanisms, based on pathways. Artif. Intell. Med. **49**(3), 135–143 (2010)

95. A. Jebali, H. Alouane, B. Atidel, P. Ladet, Operating rooms scheduling. Int. J. Prod. Econ. **99**(1–2), 52–62 (2006)

96. E. Joffe, O. Havakuk, J. Herskovic, V. Patel, E. Bernstam, Collaborative knowledge acquisition for the design of context-aware alert systems. J. Am. Med. Inform. Assoc. **19**(6), 988–994 (2012)

97. H. Kahramanli, N. Allahverdi, Design of a hybrid system for the diabetes and heart diseases. Expert Syst. Appl. 35(1–2), 82–89 (2008)

98. B.-Y. Kang, D.-W. Kim, H.-G. Kim, Two-phase chief complaint mapping to the UMLS metathesaurus in Korean electronic medical records. IEEE Trans. Inf. Technol. Biomed. **13**(1), 78–86 (2009)

99. S. Kara, B. Aksebzeci, H. Kodaz, S. Güneş, E. Kaya, H. Özbilge, Medical application of information gain-based artificial immune recognition system (IG-AIRS): classification of microorganism species. Expert Syst. Appl. **36**(3), 5168–5172 (2009)

100. M. Khalilia, S. Chakraborty, M. Popescu, Predicting disease risks from highly imbalanced data using random forest. BMC Med. Inform. Decis. Mak. **11**(51), 1–13 (2011)

101. S.E. Kimes, Yield management: a tool for capacity-considered service firms. J. Oper. Manag. **8**(4), 348–363 (1989)

102. K. Kira, L.A. Rendell, A practical approach to feature selection, in *Proceedings of the 9th International Conference on Machine Learning*, Aberdeen, 1992, pp. 249–256

103. J. Kittler, M. Hatef, R. Duin, J. Matas, On combining classifiers. IEEE Trans. Pattern Anal. Mach. Intell. **20**(3), 226–239 (1998)

104. H. Kodaz, S. Özşen, A. Arslan, S. Güneş, Medical application of information gain based artificial immune recognition system (AIRS): diagnosis of thyroid disease. Expert Syst. Appl. **36**(2), 3086–3092 (2009)

105. R. Kohavi, G. John, Wrappers for feature subset selection. Artif. Intell. **97**(1–2), 273–324 (1997)

106. A. Kolker, *Healthcare Management Engineering: What Does This Fancy Term Really Mean?* Springer Briefs in Health Care Management and Economics (Springer, New York, 2012)

107. I. Kononenko, Machine learning for medical diagnosis: history, state of the art and perspective. Artif. Intell. Med. **23**(1), 89–109 (2001)

108. P. Kralj Novak, N. Lavrač, D. Gamberger, A. Krstačić, CSM-SD: methodology for contrast set mining through subgroup discovery. J. Biomed. Inform. **42**(1), 113–122 (2009)

109. M. Krizmaric, M. Verlic, G. Stiglic, S. Grmec, P. Kokol, Intelligent analysis in predicting outcome of out-of-hospital cardiac arrest. Comput. Methods Programs Biomed. **95**(2), 22–32 (2009)

110. S. Kumar, M. Madheswaran, An improved medical decision support system to identify the diabetic retinopathy using fundus images. J. Med. Syst. **36**(6), 3573–3581 (2012)

111. L. Kuncheva, *Combining Pattern Classifiers* (Wiley, Hoboken, 2004)

112. D. Lambert, R. Adams, M. Emmelhainz, Supplier selection criteria in the healthcare industry: a comparison of importance and performace. J. Supply Chain Manag. **33**(1), 16–22 (1997)

113. M. Lamiri, F. Grimaud, X. Xie, Optimization methods for a stochastic surgery planning problem. Int. J. Prod. Econ. **120**(2), 400–410 (2009)

114. M. Lamiri, X. Xie, A. Dolgui, F. Grimaud, A stochastic model for operating room planning with elective and emergency demand for surgery. Eur. J. Oper. Res. **185**(3), 1026–1037 (2008)

115. M. Lamiri, X. Xie, S. Zhang, Column generation approach to operating theater planning with elective and emergency patients. IIE Trans. **40**(9), 838–852 (2008)

116. J.R. Langabeer, *Health Care Operations Management* (Jones & Bartlett, Sudbury, 2008)

117. S.-M. Lee, P. Abbott, Bayesian networks for knowledge discovery in large datasets: basics for nurse researchers. J. Biomed. Inform. **36**(4–5), 389–399 (2003)

118. T.-T. Lee, C.-Y. Liu, Y.-H. Kuo, M. Mills, J.-G. Fong, C. Hung, Application of data mining to the identification of critical factors in patient falls using a web-based reporting system. Int. J. Med. Inform. **80**(2), 141–150 (2011)

119. W.-I. Lee, B.-Y. Shih, Y.-S. Chung, The exploration of consumers' behavior in choosing hospital by the application of neural network. Expert Syst. Appl. **34**(2), 806–816 (2008)

120. D.-C. Li, C.-W. Liu, A class possibility based kernel to increase classification accuracy for small data sets using support vector machines. Expert Syst. Appl. **37**(4), 3104–3110 (2010)

121. D.-C. Li, C.-W. Liu, S. Hu, A fuzzy-based data transformation for feature extraction to increase classification performance with small medical data sets. Artif. Intell. Med. **52**(1), 45–52 (2011)

122. S.-T. Li, C.-C. Chen, F. Huang, Conceptual-driven classification for coding advise in health insurance reimbursement. Artif. Intell. Med. **51**(1), 27–41 (2011)

123. Z. Li, F. Liu, L. Antieau, Y. Cao, H. Yu, Lancet: a high precision medication event extraction system for clinical text. J. Am. Med. Inform. Assoc. **17**(5), 563–567 (2010)

124. C. Liang, L. Peng, An automated diagnosis system of liver disease using artificial immune and genetic algorithms. J. Med. Syst. **37**(2), 1–10 (2013)

125. G.J. Lim, A. Mobasher, L. Kardar, M.J. Cote, Nurse scheduling, in *Handbook of Health Care Systems Scheduling*, ed. by R. Hall. Volume 168 of Springer International Series in Operations Research & Management Science, chapter 3 (Springer, New York, 2011), pp. 31–64

126. J.-H. Lin, P. Haug, Exploiting missing clinical data in Bayesian network modeling for predicting medical problems. J. Biomed. Inform. **41**(1), 1–14 (2008)

127. F. Liou, Y. Tang, J. Chen, Detecting hospital fraud and claim abuse through diabetic outpatient services. Health Care Manag. Sci. **11**(4), 353–358 (2008)

128. F. Liu, L. Antieau, H. Yu, Toward automated consumer question answering: automatically separating consumer questions from professional questions in the healthcare domain. J. Biomed. Inform. **44**(6), 1032–1038 (2011)

129. P. Luukka, Similarity classifier in diagnosis of bladder cancer. Comput. Methods Programs Biomed. **89**(1), 43–49 (2008)

130. S. Lv, X. Wang, Y. Cui, J. Jin, Y. Sun, Y. Tang, Y. Bai, Y. Wang, L. Zhou, Application of attention network test and demographic information to detect mild cognitive impairment via combining feature selection with support vector machine. Comput. Methods Programs Biomed. **97**(1), 11–18 (2010)

131. D. Mackay, *Information Theory, Inference and Learning Algorithms* (Cambridge University Press, Cambridge, 2003)
132. I. Maglogiannis, E. Loukis, E. Zafiropoulos, A. Stasis, Support vectors machine-based identification of heart valve diseases using heart sounds. Comput. Methods Programs Biomed. **95**(1), 47–61 (2009)
133. F. Mancini, F. Sousa, F. Teixeira, A. Falcão, A. Hummel, T. da Costa, P. Calado, L. de Araújo, I. Pisa, Use of medical subject headings (MeSH) in Portuguese for categorizing web-based healthcare content. J. Biomed. Inform. **44**(2), 299–309 (2011)
134. E. Marcon, S. Kharraja, G. Simonnet, The operating theatre planning by the follow-up of the risk of no realization. Int. J. Prod. Econ. **85**(1), 83–90 (2003)
135. D. Margaritis, Learning Bayesian network model structure from data. Ph.D. thesis, School of Computer Science, Carnegie Mellon University, 2003
136. I. Marques, M. Captivo, M. Vaz Pato, An integer programming approach to elective surgery scheduling. OR Spectr. **34**(2), 407–427 (2012)
137. C. Meek, Complete orientation rules for patterns. Technical report, Carnegie Mellon University, 1995
138. N. Meskens, D. Duvivier, A. Hanset, Multi-objective operating room scheduling considering desiderata of the surgical team. Decis. Support Syst. **55**(2), 650–659 (2012)
139. K. Miettinen, M. Juhola, Classification of otoneurological cases according to Bayesian probabilistic models. J. Med. Syst. **34**(2), 119–130 (2010)
140. D. Min, Y. Yih, Scheduling elective surgery under uncertainty and downstream capacity constraints. Eur. J. Oper. Res. **206**(3), 642–652 (2010)
141. C. Morioka, S. El-Saden, W. Pope, J. Sayre, G. Duckwiler, F. Meng, A. Bui, H. Kangarloo, A methodology to integrate clinical data for the efficient assessment of brain-tumor patients. Inform. Health Soc. Care **33**(1), 55–68 (2008)
142. D. Mowery, J. Wiebe, S. Visweswaran, H. Harkema, W. Chapman, Building an automated SOAP classifier for emergency department reports. J. Biomed. Inform. **45**(1), 71–81 (2012)
143. T. Mu, T. Pataky, A. Findlow, M. Aung, J. Goulermas, Automated nonlinear feature generation and classification of foot pressure lesions. IEEE Trans. Inf. Technol. Biomed. **14**(2), 418–424 (2010)
144. R. Nagarajan, M. Scutari, S. Lèbre, *Bayesian Networks in R* (Springer, New York, 2013)
145. K. Neumann, C. Schwindt, J. Zimmermann, *Project Scheduling with Time Windows and Scarce Resources*, 2nd edn. (Springer, Berlin, 2003)
146. A. Nguyen, M. Lawley, D. Hansen, R. Bowman, B. Clarke, E. Duhig, S. Colquist, Symbolic rule-based classification of lung cancer stages from free-text pathology reports. J. Am. Med. Inform. Assoc. **17**(4), 440–445 (2010)
147. S. Ogulata, R. Erol, A hierarchical multiple criteria mathematical programming approach for scheduling general surgery operations in large hospitals. J. Med. Syst. **27**(3), 259–270 (2003)
148. J.H. Oh, P. Gurnani, J. Schorge, K.P. Rosenblatt, J.X. Gao, An extended Markov blanket approach to proteomic biomarker detection from high-resolution mass spectrometry data. IEEE Trans. Inf. Technol. Biomed. **13**(2), 195–206 (2009)
149. L. Ohno-Machado, Modeling medical prognosis: survival analysis techniques. J. Biomed. Inform. **34**(6), 428–439 (2001)
150. A. Oniśko, M. Druzdzel, Impact of precision of Bayesian network parameters on accuracy of medical diagnostic systems. Artif. Intell. Med. **57**(3), 197–206 (2013)
151. Y.A. Ozcan, *Health Care Benchmarking and Performance Evaluation*. Springer International Series in Operations Research & Management Science (Springer, New York, 2008)
152. Y.A. Ozcan, *Quantitative Methods in Health Care Management – Techniques and Applications*, 2nd edn. (Jossey-Bass, San Francisco, 2009)
153. A. Ozcift, Enhanced cancer recognition system based on random forests feature elimination algorithm. J. Med. Syst. **36**(4), 2577–2585 (2011)
154. I. Ozkarahan, Allocation of surgeries to operating rooms by goal programing. J. Med. Syst. **24**(6), 339–378 (2000)

155. A. Oztekin, D. Delen, Z.J. Kong, Predicting the graft survival for heart-lung transplantation patients: an integrated data mining methodology. Int. J. Med. Inform. **78**(12), 84–96 (2009)
156. S. Pakhomov, P. Hanson, S. Bjornsen, S. Smith, Automatic classification of foot examination findings using clinical notes and machine learning. J. Am. Med. Inform. Assoc. **15**(2), 198–202 (2008)
157. S. Parhizi, L. Steege, K. Pasupathy, Mining the relationships between psychosocial factors and fatigue dimensions among registered nurses. Int. J. Ind. Ergon. **43**(1), 82–90 (2013)
158. J. Patrick, M. Li, High accuracy information extraction of medication information from clinical notes: 2009 i2b2 medication extraction challenge. J. Am. Med. Inform. Assoc. **17**(5), 524–527 (2010)
159. J. Patrick, D. Nguyen, Y. Wang, M. Li, A knowledge discovery and reuse pipeline for information extraction in clinical notes. J. Am. Med. Inform. Assoc. **18**(5), 574–579 (2011)
160. J. Pearl, *Causality: Models, Reasoning and Inference* (Cambridge University Press, Cambridge, 2000)
161. L. Pecchia, P. Melillo, M. Sansone, M. Bracale, Discrimination power of short-term heart rate variability measures for CHF assessment. IEEE Trans. Inf. Technol. Biomed. **15**(1), 40–46 (2011)
162. C. Perlich, F. Provost, J. Simonoff, Tree induction vs. logistic regression: a learning-curve analysis. J. Mach. Learn. Res. **4**(1), 211–255 (2003)
163. M. Persson, J. Persson, Analysing management policies for operating room planning using simulation. Health Care Manag. Sci. **13**(2), 182–191 (2010)
164. P. Petrantonakis, L. Hadjileontiadis, Emotion recognition from EEG using higher order crossings. IEEE Trans. Inf. Technol. Biomed. **14**(2), 186–197 (2010)
165. D.N. Pham, A. Klinkert, Surgical case scheduling as a generalized job shop scheduling problem. Eur. J. Oper. Res. **185**(3), 1011–1025 (2008)
166. V. Podgorelec, P. Kokol, Genetic algorithm based system for patient scheduling in highly constrained situations. J. Med. Syst. **21**(6), 417–427 (1997)
167. V. Podgorelec, P. Kokol, B. Stiglic, I. Rozman, Decision trees: an overview and their use in medicine. J. Med. Syst. **26**(5), 445–463 (2002)
168. K. Polat, Application of attribute weighting method based on clustering centers to discrimination of linearly non-separable medical datasets. J. Med. Syst. **36**(4), 2657–2673 (2011)
169. K. Polat, S. Güneş, A new feature selection method on classification of medical datasets: Kernel F-score feature selection. Expert Syst. Appl. **36**(7), 10367–10373 (2009)
170. K. Polat, S. Kara, A. Güven, S. Güneş, Usage of class dependency based feature selection and fuzzy weighted pre-processing methods on classification of macular disease. Expert Syst. Appl. **36**(2), 2584–2591 (2009)
171. J. Pollettini, S. Panico, J. Daneluzzi, R. Tinós, J. Baranauskas, A. MacEdo, Using machine learning classifiers to assist healthcare-related decisions: classification of electronic patient records. J. Med. Syst. **36**(6), 3861–3874 (2012)
172. M. Porter, C. Guth, *Redefining German Health Care – Moving to a Value-Based System* (Springer, Heidelberg, 2012)
173. A.A.B. Pritsker, L. Watters, P.M. Wolfe, Multiproject scheduling with limited resources: a zero-one programming approach. Manag. Sci. **16**(1), 93–108 (1969)
174. X. Qu, Y. Peng, N. Kong, J. Shi, A two-phase approach to scheduling multi-category outpatient appointments – a case study of a women's clinic. Health Care Manag. Sci. **16**(2), 1–20 (2013)
175. J. Quinlan, *C4.5: Programs for Machine Learning* (Morgan Kaufman, San Mateo, 1992)
176. R. Ramiarina, R. Almeida, W. Pereira, Hospital costs estimation and prediction as a function of patient and admission characteristics. Int. J. Health Plan. Manag. **23**(4), 345–355 (2007)
177. J. Ramsey, A PC-style Markov blanket search for high dimensional datasets. Technical report, Carnegie Mellon University, 2006
178. J. Rasku, H. Joutsijoki, I. Pyykkö, M. Juhola, Prediction of a state of a subject on the basis of a stabilogram signal and video oculography test. Comput. Methods Programs Biomed. **108**(2), 580–588 (2012)

179. A. Razavi, H. Gill, H. Ahlfeldt, N. Shahsavar, Non-compliance with a postmastectomy radiotherapy guideline: decision tree and cause analysis. BMC Med. Inform. Decis. Mak. **8**(41), 1–8 (2008)

180. P. Revesz, T. Triplet, Classification integration and reclassification using constraint databases. Artif. Intell. Med. **49**(2), 79–91 (2010)

181. A. Riise, E. Burke, Local search for the surgery admission planning problem. J. Heuristics **17**(4), 389–414 (2011)

182. B. Rink, S. Harabagiu, K. Roberts, Automatic extraction of relations between medical concepts in clinical texts. J. Am. Med. Inform. Assoc. **18**(5), 594–600 (2011)

183. K. Roberts, S. Harabagiu, A flexible framework for deriving assertions from electronic medical records. J. Am. Med. Inform. Assoc. **18**(5), 568–573 (2011)

184. M. Robnik-Šikonja, I. Kononenko, Theoretical and empirical analysis of ReliefF and RReliefF. Mach. Learn. **53**(1), 23–69 (2003)

185. F. Rogers, T. Osler, S. Shackford, M. Cohen, L. Camp, Financial outcome of treating trauma in a rural environment. J. Trauma **43**(1), 65–73 (1997)

186. B. Roland, C. Di Martinelly, F. Riane, Y. Pochet, Scheduling an operating theatre under human resource constraints. Comput. Ind. Eng. **58**(2), 212–220 (2010)

187. Y. Roumani, J. May, D. Strum, L. Vargas, Classifying highly imbalanced ICU data. Health Care Manag. Sci. **16**(2), 119–128 (2013)

188. S. Rubrichi, S. Quaglini, Summary of product characteristics content extraction for a safe drugs usage. J. Biomed. Inform. **45**(2), 231–239 (2012)

189. M. Sariyar, A. Borg, Bagging, bumping, multiview, and active learning for record linkage with empirical results on patient identity data. Comput. Methods Programs Biomed. **108**(3), 1160–1169 (2012)

190. M. Sariyar, A. Borg, K. Pommerening, Evaluation of record linkage methods for iterative insertions. Methods Inf. Med. **48**(5), 429–437 (2009)

191. M. Sariyar, A. Borg, K. Pommerening, Active learning strategies for the deduplication of electronic patient data using classification trees. J. Biomed. Inform. **45**(5), 893–900 (2012)

192. M. Sariyar, A. Borg, K. Pommerening, Missing values in deduplication of electronic patient data. J. Am. Med. Inform. Assoc. **19**(1), 76–82 (2012)

193. K. Schimmelpfeng, S. Helber, S. Kasper, Decision support for rehabilitation hospital scheduling. OR Spectr. **34**(2), 461–489 (2012)

194. J. Schreyögg, T. Stargardt, O. Tiemann, R. Busse, Methods to determine reimbursement rates for diagnosis related groups (DRG): a comparison of nine European countries. Health Care Manag. Sci. **9**(3), 215–223 (2006)

195. J. Schreyögg, O. Tiemann, R. Busse, Cost accounting to determine prices: how well do prices reflect costs in the German DRG-system? Health Care Manag. Sci. **9**(3), 269–279 (2006)

196. H.-J. Schütz, R. Kolisch, Approximate dynamic programming for capacity allocation in the service industry. Eur. J. Oper. Res. **218**(1), 239–250 (2012)

197. J. Schulenburg, M. Blanke, *Rationing of Medical Services in Europe: An Empirical Study* (IOS Press, Amsterdam, 2004)

198. M. Scotch, M. Duggal, C. Brandt, Z. Lin, R. Shiffman, Use of statistical analysis in the biomedical informatics literature. J. Am. Med. Inform. Assoc. **17**(1), 3–5 (2010)

199. M. Scutari, Learning Bayesian networks with the bnlearn package. J. Stat. Softw. **35**(3), 1–22 (2010)

200. M. Scutari, K. Strimmer, Introduction to graphical modelling, in *Handbook of Statistical Systems Biology*, chapter 11, ed. by M. Stumpf, D. Balding, M. Girolami (Wiley, Chichester, 2010), pp. 235–254

201. J.A. Sepulveda, Prospective payment: a simulation model of management strategies, in *Proceedings of the 17th Conference on Winter Simulation*, San Francisco, 1985, pp. 532–540

202. R. Shanmugam, A diagnostic methodology for hazy data with "borderline" cases. J. Med. Syst. **34**(2), 161–177 (2010)

203. Y. Shao, J. Bard, A. Jarrah, The therapist routing and scheduling problem. IIE Trans. (Institute of Industrial Engineers) **44**(10), 868–893 (2012)

204. A. Sharma, Inter-DRG resource dynamics in a prospective payment system: a stochastic kernel approach. Health Care Manag. Sci. **12**(1), 38–55 (2009)
205. M.J. Sharma, S.J. Yu, Benchmark optimization and attribute identification for improvement of container terminals. Eur. J. Oper. Res. **201**(2), 568–580 (2009)
206. J.M. Shiver, D. Eitel, *Optimizing Emergency Department Throughput* (Taylor & Francis, New York, 2010)
207. A. Smith, C. Nugent, S. McClean, Evaluation of inherent performance of intelligent medical decision support systems: utilising neural networks as an example. Artif. Intell. Med. **27**(1), 1–27 (2003)
208. Z. Song, Z. Ji, J.-G. Ma, B. Sputh, U. Acharya, O. Faust, A systematic approach to embedded biomedical decision making. Comput. Methods Programs Biomed. **108**(2), 656–664 (2012)
209. N. Sriraam, EEG based automated detection of auditory loss: a pilot study. Expert Syst. Appl. **39**(1), 723–731 (2012)
210. I. Štajduhar, B. Dalbelo-Bašić, Learning Bayesian networks from survival data using weighting censored instances. J. Biomed. Inform. **43**(4), 613–622 (2010)
211. I. Štajduhar, B. Dalbelo-Bašić, Uncensoring censored data for machine learning: a likelihood-based approach. Expert Syst. Appl. **39**(8), 7226–7234 (2012)
212. R. Stoean, C. Stoean, Modeling medical decision making by support vector machines, explaining by rules of evolutionary algorithms with feature selection. Expert Syst. Appl. **40**(7), 2677–2686 (2013)
213. R. Stoean, C. Stoean, M. Lupsor, H. Stefanescu, R. Badea, Evolutionary-driven support vector machines for determining the degree of liver fibrosis in chronic hepatitis C. Artif. Intell. Med. **51**(1), 53–65 (2011)
214. N. Sut, O. Simsek, Comparison of regression tree data mining methods for prediction of mortality in head injury. Expert Syst. Appl. **38**(12), 15534–15539 (2011)
215. M. Tagluk, N. Sezgin, M. Akin, Estimation of sleep stages by an artificial neural network employing EEG, EMG and EOG. J. Med. Syst. **34**(4), 717–725 (2010)
216. A. Testi, E. Tánfani, Tactical and operational decisions for operating room planning: efficiency and welfare implications. Health Care Manag. Sci. **12**(4), 363–373 (2009)
217. M. Testik, B. Ozkaya, S. Aksu, O. Ozcebe, Discovering blood donor arrival patterns using data mining: a method to investigate service quality at blood centers. J. Med. Syst. **36**(2), 579–594 (2012)
218. I. Tsamardinos, C. Aliferis, A. Statnikov, Algorithms for large scale Markov blanket discovery, in *Proceedings of the 16th International Florida Artificial Intelligence Research Society Conference*, St. Augustine, 2003, pp 376–381
219. K. Tufan, S. Kara, F. Latifoglu, S. Aydin, A. Kiriş, U. Özkuvanci, Non-invasive diagnosis of stress urinary incontinence sub types using wavelet analysis, shannon entropy and principal component analysis. J. Med. Syst. **36**(4), 2159–2169 (2012)
220. E. Übeyli, K. Ilbay, G. Ilbay, D. Sahin, G. Akansel, Differentiation of two subtypes of adult hydrocephalus by mixture of experts. J. Med. Syst. **34**(3), 281–290 (2010)
221. O. Uzuner, J. Mailoa, R. Ryan, T. Sibanda, Semantic relations for problem-oriented medical records. Artif. Intell. Med. **50**(2), 63–73 (2010)
222. P.T. Vanberkel, R.J. Boucherie, E.W. Hans, J.L. Hurink, N. Litvak, A survey of health care models that encompass multiple departments. Int. J. Health Manag. Inf. **1**(1), 37–69 (2010)
223. B. Van Calster, G. Condous, E. Kirk, T. Bourne, D. Timmerman, S. Van Huffel, An application of methods for the probabilistic three-class classification of pregnancies of unknown location. Artif. Intell. Med. **46**(2), 139–154 (2009)
224. J. van de Klundert, P. Gorissen, S. Zeemering, Measuring clinical pathway adherence. J. Biomed. Inform. **43**(6), 861–872 (2010)
225. K. Varpa, K. Iltanen, M. Juhola, Machine learning method for knowledge discovery experimented with otoneurological data. Comput. Methods Programs Biomed. **91**(2), 154–164 (2008)
226. C. Vidrighin, R. Potolea, Proicet: a cost-sensitive system for prostate cancer data. Health Inform. J. **14**(4), 297–307 (2008)

227. B. Vijayakumar, P. Parikh, R. Scott, A. Barnes, J. Gallimore, A dual bin-packing approach to scheduling surgical cases at a publicly-funded hospital. Eur. J. Oper. Res. **224**(3), 583–591 (2013)
228. J. Vissers, I. Adan, J. Bekkers, Patient mix optimization in tactical cardiothoracic surgery planning: a case study. IMA J. Manag. Math. **16**(3), 281–304 (2005)
229. J. Vissers, R. Beech, *Health Operations Management: Patient Flow Logistics in Health Care* (Routledge, New York, 2005)
230. K. Wagholikar, S. Mangrulkar, A. Deshpande, V. Sundararajan, Evaluation of fuzzy relation method for medical decision support. J. Med. Syst. **36**(1), 233–239 (2012)
231. L. Wasserman, *All of Statistics: A Concise Course in Statistical Inference* (Springer, New York, 2004)
232. R. Wicentowski, M. Sydes, Using implicit information to identify smoking status in smoke-blind medical discharge summaries. J. Am. Med. Inform. Assoc. **15**(1), 29–31 (2008)
233. I. Witten, E. Frank, *Data Mining: Practical Machine Learning Tools and Techniques*, 2nd edn. (Morgan Kaufmann, San Francisco, 2005)
234. J. Wu, J. Roy, W. Stewart, Prediction modeling using EHR data: challenges, strategies, and a comparison of machine learning approaches. Med. Care **48**(6), 106–113 (2010)
235. Y. Xu, K. Hong, J. Tsujii, E.-C. Chang, Feature engineering combined with machine learning and rule-based methods for structured information extraction from narrative clinical discharge summaries. J. Am. Med. Inform. Assoc. **19**(5), 824–832 (2012)
236. Y. Xu, J. Liu, J. Wu, Y. Wang, Z. Tu, J.-T. Sun, J. Tsujii, E.-C. Chang, A classification approach to coreference in discharge summaries: 2011 i2b2 challenge. J. Am. Med. Inform. Assoc. **19**(5), 897–905 (2012)
237. Q. Yan, H. Yan, F. Han, X. Wei, T. Zhu, SVM-based decision support system for clinic aided tracheal intubation predication with multiple features. Expert Syst. Appl. **36**(3), 6588–6592 (2009)
238. Y. Yih, *Handbook of Healthcare Delivery Systems* (CRC, Boca Raton, 2011)
239. L. Yu, H. Liu, Efficient feature selection via analysis of relevance and redundancy. J. Mach. Learn. Res. **5**(1), 1205–1224 (2004)
240. M. Yu, A. Rhuma, S. Naqvi, L. Wang, J. Chambers, A posture recognition-based fall detection system for monitoring an elderly person in a smart home environment. IEEE Trans. Inf. Technol. Biomed. **16**(6), 1274–1286 (2012)
241. F. Zakeri, H. Behnam, N. Ahmadinejad, Classification of benign and malignant breast masses based on shape and texture features in sonography images. J. Med. Syst. **36**(3), 1621–1627 (2012)
242. M. Zaugg, A. Gattiker, C. Moneta, T. Reay, Effective leadership in hospital management: how a CEO can lead a hospital towards more "competitiveness". The GZO case in Switzerland. Online J. Int. Case Anal. **3**(1), 1–24 (2012)
243. W. Zelman, M. McCue, A. Millikan, N. Glick, *Financial Management of Health Care Organizations: An Introduction to Fundamental Tools, Concepts and Applications* (Wiley-Blackwell, Malden, 2002)
244. J. Zheng, W. Chapman, T. Miller, C. Lin, R. Crowley, G. Savova, A system for coreference resolution for the clinical narrative. J. Am. Med. Inform. Assoc. **19**(4), 660–667 (2012)
245. W. Zhong, R. Chow, J. He, Clinical charge profiles prediction for patients diagnosed with chronic diseases using multi-level support vector machine. Expert Syst. Appl. **39**(1), 1474–1483 (2012)
246. X. Zhou, S. Chen, B. Liu, R. Zhang, Y. Wang, P. Li, Y. Guo, H. Zhang, Z. Gao, X. Yan, Development of traditional chinese medicine clinical data warehouse for medical knowledge discovery and decision support. Artif. Intell. Med. **48**(2–3), 139–152 (2010)